SHAKESPEARE AND THE STUDENTS

SHAKESPEARE
AND
THE STUDENTS

By

D. J. Enright

1970

CHATTO & WINDUS

LONDON

Published by
Chatto & Windus Ltd
40 William IV Street
London W.C.2.

*

Clarke, Irwin & Co. Ltd
Toronto

SBN 7011 1567 x cloth edn.
SBN 7011 1568 8 paper edn.

Printed in Great Britain by
R. & R. Clark, Ltd., Edinburgh

Read him therefore; and again, and again.
And if then you do not like him, surely you are
in some manifest danger, not to understand him
Heminge and Condell,
Preface to the First Folio, 1623.

CONTENTS

INTRODUCTION

THIS book has arisen directly out of teaching the four plays, *King Lear*, *Antony and Cleopatra*, *Macbeth* and *The Winter's Tale*: that is to say, out of a fairly intimate acquaintance not only with students' difficulties but also (and more so) with the things they find all too easy. The difficulties are generally legitimate and can usually be dealt with. The easinesses, which are illegitimate, are less readily dealt with, because inevitably one seems to be snatching from one's hard-pressed pupils the manna dropped around them by the godlike critics, urging them the while to act like noble savages, nakedly confronting the bleak text, when they would much prefer to be less noble and more civilised.

In the first edition of *The Wheel of Fire*, that influential book on the interpretation of Shakespearean tragedy, G. Wilson Knight asserted that the persons, the characters of the plays, 'ultimately, are not human at all, but purely symbols of a poetic vision'. An unhappy consequence of this view of Shakespeare has been to make of his work an academic subject, remote from the merely 'human' concerns of the student. Many students have all too swiftly taken a further tip from L. C. Knights's reference to 'the necessary aloofness from a work of art', and art is then seen to be about what happened to *other* people —or better still, not to people at all, but just to symbols. Literature becomes something you are examined in at the end of the course, and you remain aloof from it at least until that grim day arrives with its inhuman concerns.

M. C. Bradbrook once wrote, 'It is in the total situation rather than in the wrigglings of individual emotion that the tragedy lies.' One sees what she meant. But too often

9

—for how many students will strive in the face of such discouragement to establish the 'total situation' for themselves?—this piece of advice has been construed as an excuse for not bothering with the uncomfortably complex wrigglings of Macbeth or Antony. The necessity of what we can still call 'modern' Shakespearean criticism cannot be denied. But there must be other teachers besides myself who feel that we have been rescued from the smoke and fire of romanticism only to be dropped into the hygienic incinerators of symbolism, imagery-computation, a curiously trite moralising, and philosophising of a sort so primitive as undoubtedly to have contributed to the discredit which literature has fallen into among the serious-minded. If in the heat of his excitement A. C. Bradley occasionally gets between us and Shakespeare, yet he never obscures for long what he purposes to reveal; he sometimes expands the text into thin air, but he doesn't reduce it; he may distort, but he never belittles, for his commentary invariably makes you feel that at least the text is worth reading.

So often the teacher sees that personal involvement in a play is being discouraged either by the student's modesty (who is he to set up in competition with the famous exegetes?) and the respect which his other studies have inculcated in him for scientific-sounding formulations and jargon, or else of course by his lazy pragmatism (why struggle with the play when you can take over someone else's tidy résumé of it?). And so a student who has passed up a very knowledgeable essay on the reversal or the violation of the natural order in *Macbeth*, involving the Great Chain of Being, the Elizabethan World Picture and other such handy encapsulations, is nevertheless found incapable of paraphrasing a passage from the play however crudely.

The formulae popularised by some modern critics are conveniently capacious, and far from serving to distinguish one play from another, to describe the thisness of a particular work, their effect is to make all the plays sound much of a muchness. The commentator who tells us that the conversation between Rosse and the Old Man in *Macbeth* is a projection of disorder in the state says exactly the same thing about the goings-on in the Boar's Head Tavern in *Henry IV*. Surely a formula which proposes to tell us something about two such dissimilar matters is unlikely to tell us anything that really counts about either? Yet so seductive is this quasi-metaphysical formulation that I have seen the expressions 'inversion of values' and 'violation of the natural order' slopping over from the Shakespeare course and being applied to Eve's eating of the apple and what ensues in *Paradise Lost* and also to such lines in *The Rape of the Lock* as 'Puffs, Powders, Patches, Bibles, Billet-doux'.

We should not be too quick to blame the critics for this state of affairs, and we must grant that those critics who are out of fashion are obviously likely to do the least harm. Moreover, we have been warned—if sometimes in a whisper. We believe Professor Wilson Knight when he says, in a prefatory note to later editions of *The Wheel of Fire*, that 'my animadversions as to "character" analysis were never intended to limit the living human reality of Shakespeare's people'. Mr. Traversi has admitted that 'abstract profundities' are misleading in the discussion of Shakespeare's 'symbolism'. And Professor Knights has told us that 'we should remember . . . that the life of the imagination runs deeper than our conscious formulations'. But such scruples are easily disregarded as mere pedantry, and what happens is that the more or less complex formula of the original critic—complex but still a formula —is reduced by teacher and then by pupil to an ever simpler formula. The complex formulation may send you back to the play—indeed, you cannot *understand* much of the best commentary without studying the text alongside!

—but the simple formulation, such is simplicity's charm, does no such thing: it simply usurps the play. The stimulant has turned into a bromide; the proof of the pudding has come to reside in a stock recipe.

Another present disorder lies in the tendency among critics and teachers—and then among students—to find fault with Shakespeare, I mean with Shakespeare at his greatest; or rather, to hunt for faults, to niggle and carp in an ingenious though peculiarly graceless fashion. This tendency, I am pretty sure, grows out of the necessity which most academics experience at some time of lecturing or writing on Shakespeare combined with their natural desire to say something new, to produce an effect. It may sometimes have to do with a feeling of resentment: no one can be *that* good, least of all a writer whose works, as they devolved from one generation to another, have received new honours at every transmission—in which case Johnson's words about those who, 'being able to add nothing to truth, hope for eminence from the heresies of paradox' may be thought to apply. Either way, misunderstandings are not met with, or innocently incurred through that frailty common to us all, so much as avidly courted, willed into being for the purpose of exploitation. For this reason I chose my epigraph from Shakespeare's first editors: 'Read him, therefore; and again, and again . . .', for as regards these four plays of his, I feel with Hazlitt that 'our admiration cannot easily surpass his genius'.

If commentary is so pernicious, it may be asked, then why propose to add to it? In extenuation I could cite Pope's remark that, even so, 'of all English Poets Shakespeare must be confessed to be the fairest and fullest subject for criticism'. I could quote John Middleton Murry's comment, as he fought his way through an interpretation of Shakespeare, that 'like the lated traveller, I spur apace to gain the timely inn: which in this case is, happily enough the plain text of Shakespeare', and add that, much as one sympathises with Murry, the fact remains that what is plain to one man is not plain in the least to the next. More to the point, I could submit that a procedure as rebarbative as the running (or stumbling) commentaries which follow is so utterly lacking in seductive power as to drive even the most susceptible student back to the texts.

*   *   *

I am indebted to the critics I have disagreed with (as regards the others, one can only plead that many excellent and true things have been said of Shakespeare and later writers are bound to repeat some of them), to the students who have helped to enforce a recognition of how potent criticism can be, and to the editors of the Arden editions of the plays, which I have followed throughout. And of course, like the rest of us, to Shakespeare.

'KING LEAR'
and the Just Gods

'KING LEAR'
AND THE JUST GODS

THE first part of the first scene of the play conveys an item of information (the kingdom is to be divided) and explains the nature of Edmund's birth. One might have expected Kent to know about the latter, for Shakespeare's courts are generally much given to gossip, and perhaps Gloucester's remark that Edmund has 'been out nine years', a débutante in reverse, is a casual sop to credulity or 'realism'. But chiefly the scene is of interest because of the economical insight it provides into the disposition of Gloucester himself: he is going to feature importantly and (I think) impressively in the play, and it is pertinent that we should meet him at the outset, before we meet Lear, and that we should meet him at his least likeable.

Gloucester is obviously tickled by the thought of his prowess in begetting a bastard son, long ago though it was. We don't imagine for a moment that he has 'often blush'd to acknowledge' Edmund, except to blush with self-pleasure. The crude and self-congratulatory pun on the word 'conceive' underlines this impression. At the same time, 'Do you smell a fault?' he asks, perhaps a little nervously—for Kent is such a gentleman—but more likely in the expectation of a flattering response implying the answer 'On the contrary'. Being a gentleman, Kent supplies it, in a nicely turned compliment to Edmund ('the issue of it being so proper') which is going to be sadly discredited: this is the play's first misjudgment.

'There was good sport at his making,' babbles Gloucester, 'and the whoreson must be acknowledged.' It occurs to us that in any contest between the two sons, Gloucester could well be swayed in favour of Edmund as the token of his former virility, a gay young spark reflecting a gay old one. Edmund's closing civility, 'I shall study deserving', is apt in the sense that he will deserve studying; he is one of Shakespeare's richest villains, and we come to see that Gloucester does have reason for 'preferring' him to Edgar quite aside from his senile self-satisfaction. Edgar is rather a dry stick, he has to tell himself what he should feel, and there is a good deal more priggishness in his composition than can be justified by the accident of legitimacy. However, as one of my students once put it, Gloucester is due for an eye-opener before long.

Incidentally, according to G. Wilson Knight, 'the first sentence of the play suggests that Lear is guilty of bias',* when Kent says, 'I thought the King had more affected the Duke of Albany than Cornwall.' Yet surely a king may be allowed to prefer one of his sons-in-law, one of his heirs, to another? Furthermore, if what Kent says is true, then Lear was right in his original preference. We are not meant to regard him as a cretin.

Multum in parvo, in some thirty lines. Then enter the main figures of the main plot, and Lear at once broaches what he very aptly calls his 'darker purpose'. It is dark to his court, it is also dark to himself. He has yielded to the romantic notion of retirement from this vale of tears and trivialities, the notion of emulating some oriental despot who hands over the crown and all his power and repairs to a mountainous cell where in due time he will acquire a new name and authority as a holy man and wise guru. It is a dream, or a fairy-tale, and Lear is in no way fitted for renunciation of worldly power, any more than in his present condition he is fitted for a career of unworldly wisdom. He is proposing to give up something he is apparently fairly good at—ruling a prehistoric Britain—

* 'The *Lear* Universe', *The Wheel of Fire*, 1930.

for something which indeed he has taken too little care of.

> . . . 'tis our fast intent
> To shake all cares and business from our age,
> Conferring them on younger strengths, while we
> Unburthen'd crawl toward death

—this is a quite superb misstatement of what is to happen: for Lear is about to acquire some truly heavy burdens and to be driven fast towards death. Chiefly, of course, we notice the sustained regality of his bearing at a time when he is supposedly renouncing his regal status. This is a man who is far from ready to crawl towards death or anything else, a man who will have to be beaten to his knees (by the use of quite specific force) and to what holiness he can achieve in that position.

The 'contest' among the daughters is faked, in that their portions are already marked out for them, with the largest left to the last for the favourite child, and so it doesn't much matter what Goneril and Regan say as long as they say they love their father. Regan goes one better than Goneril, in the crude manner of 'the same with knobs on', and she gets an 'ample third of our fair kingdom' ('no less . . . Than that conferr'd on Goneril'), a third in the sense perhaps that all three thirds of England are naturally ample, though one of them ('a third more opulent') is more ample than the other two.

It is difficult, in what follows, to be fair to both Lear and Cordelia. But one must try to be. Lear does love Cordelia more than his other daughters—his much complained-of judgment is not all that faulty—and he has reserved the lion's share for her as well as 'her kind nursery' for himself. He knows in advance that she loves him more than do the other daughters. His misjudgment is in believing that she will express her love in this public competition, and in trying to force her to do so. How bad a misjudgment

is this? Even in full knowledge of a person's fastidiousness, one can still expect or hope that the person will
thrust aside this fastidiousness (even though it is part of
the reason for loving her) and simply express *the truth*.
'If you love me, then say so, even though you know that
words are cheap': after all, sillier love-tests have been set
than this.

Lear's fury is easily accounted for. The father has been
betrayed for the sake of a scruple: we cannot believe that
Lucasta would have been other than resentful had the
poet announced publicly that he loved Honour more. And
the King has been humiliated in public, with the map of
Britain already hung, drawn and quartered in front of the
assembly. 'Nothing will come of nothing: speak again':
he gives Cordelia fair warning; she should not be in-
fluenced by the behaviour of her sisters, she should love
him too much to be struck dumb by their facileness. That
of course we are of Cordelia's party on principle (principles
don't have much to do with love) should not lead us to see
Lear as a senile tyrant: we should leave that to Goneril and
Regan, whose vision readily accommodates itself to their
ambitions. Coleridge noted, as have later critics, that Cordelia's tone 'is well contrived to lessen the glaring absurdity of Lear's conduct'.

In this somewhat hectic atmosphere, Cordelia reveals
herself a true Englishman:

> *Unhappy that I am, I cannot heave*
> *My heart into my mouth: I love your Majesty*
> *According to my bond; no more nor less.*

We should think less of her if she could heave her heart
into her mouth; but then, we are not her father—a father,
incidentally, with no sons and no wife. Perhaps, along with
Derek Traversi, we could give the word 'bond' a less
legalistic, much richer significance, inclusive of devotion
and love: that which you are 'bound' to feel, being such a

KING LEAR

daughter of such a father, as well as that which you are
'bonded' to feel. But no, it is an irredeemably cold word,
it has little visible connection with the love Lear means,
and we cannot expect him to stop dead and embark on a
sympathetic analysis of what it *might* mean. In some of her
curt pronouncements, Cordelia is not so far removed
from Blake's 'Little Boy Lost', who says,

> *'Nought loves another as itself,*
> *Nor venerates another so . . .*
>
> *And Father, how can I love you*
> *Or any of my brothers more?'*

and is thereupon seized by the Priest:

> *'Lo, what a fiend is here!' said he,*
> *'One who sets reason up for judge*
> *Of our most holy Mystery.'*

For she is excessively reasonable in her mode of dealing
with mysterious matters. But perhaps A. C. Bradley's
comment is the most fitting as it is certainly the most
humane: 'Even if truth *were* the one and only obligation,
to tell much less than the truth is not to tell it.'*

Exercising a restraint which we later realise is quite remarkable for him, Lear gives her a further chance to
swallow her pride and please him. But she answers,

> *Good my Lord,*
> *You have begot me, bred me, lov'd me: I*
> *Return those duties back as are right fit,*
> *Obey you, love you, and most honour you . . .*

Again she equates love with a colder concept, that of duty,
and possibly implies (for the words can be read another
way) that her father was only doing his duty in loving her.
She then continues,

> *Why have my sisters husbands, if they say*
> *They love you all? Happily, when I shall wed,*

* *Shakespearean Tragedy*, 1904.

21

That lord whose hand must take my plight shall carry
Half my love with him, half my care and duty:
Sure I shall never marry like my sisters,   ·
To love my father all.

This is excellent sense, of course; yet Goneril and Regan *are* pleasing their husbands, ostensibly doing their duty to their partners, by bringing home ample thirds of the kingdom. Cordelia's account of matrimony, even if it is indebted to the marriage service, has something of the air of a debating point about it. In any case, as far as *she* is concerned, she is not married yet, so the question of her matrimonial feelings is irrelevant, unless we assume that (fortunately) she has fallen in love with France already. What she is doing here is attacking her sisters' position rather than defending her own.

'So young, and so untender?' Lear asks incredulously. And her answer (more than our father is our honesty) smacks of priggishness: 'So young, my Lord, and true.' How could Lear deny himself the obvious rejoinder, 'thy truth then be thy dower'? This is a domestic flare-up, but we think of Polixenes' comment on a domestic disorder in *The Winter's Tale*:

>   *This jealousy*
> *Is for a precious creature: as she's rare,*
> *Must it be great; and, as his person's mighty,*
> *Must it be violent . . .*

A domestic matter, yes, but when Professor Wilson Knight says, 'It is, indeed, curious that so storm-furious a play as *King Lear* should have so trivial a domestic basis: it is the first of our many incongruities to be noticed',* we cannot but reply that there is nothing curious about that, and no incongruity forces itself upon our notice when a storm that begins at home ends on the heath. The

* '*King Lear* and the Comedy of the Grotesque', *The Wheel of Fire*.

members of this family are not squabbling about the colour of the curtains or whether they should have fish or meat for lunch.

In his solemn renunciation of Cordelia, Lear huffs and puffs somewhat ('The barbarous Scythian . . .'), but the curse is nothing like as hate-filled and horrifying as his later curses are to be.

> *I lov'd her most, and thought to set my rest*
> *On her kind nursery. Hence, and avoid my sight!*

—hell hath no fury like anybody scorned. Students, the young, are all too ready to dismiss Lear as a rash and senile dodderer, in which they are at one with the presumably fairly youthful Goneril and Regan, and it seems necessary to point out that in fact his behaviour is not egregiously eccentric or absurd.* At no point does one's consciousness of his wrongness drive out one's recognition of the pathos of the situation, of the real anguish which (however idiotic the love-contest) Lear is experiencing. Far from senile, he is alive at every moment; and if we weep, we weep for him, more than for Cordelia.

The decisiveness of his language in handing over power is quite impressive, and of course ironically royal. So, I think we should admit, is his first reaction to Kent's intercession: 'Come not between the Dragon and his wrath': and his later warning: 'The bow is bent and drawn; make from the shaft.' Kent's 'unmannerly' speech is the more effective for the gentlemanliness we have hitherto noted in him: 'What would'st thou do, old man?' This is the sort of language which Lear is soon to hear on the lips of his loving daughters.

---

* Nothing of interest about the play can be said by anyone who believes, with Jan Kott (*Shakespeare Our Contemporary*, 1964), that 'regarded as a person, a character, Lear is ridiculous, naive and stupid', and manages to preserve that belief.

23

What follows—France's formal speech,

> *This is most strange,*
> *That she, whom even but now was your best object,*
> *The argument of your praise, balm of your age,*
> *The best, the dearest, should in this trice of time*
> *Commit a thing so monstrous, to dismantle*
> *So many folds of favour,*

and Cordelia's slightly snappish and Pharisaic speech about her want of 'such a tongue That I am glad I have not'—is necessary to the proper progress of the story. France is not to marry an unchaste murderess, he must love and respect Cordelia, he must judge her (and be seen to judge her) worth marrying for herself alone, if only to obviate any suggestion of expansionist designs on Britain when his troops appear at Dover. In that matter he is pitying her tears, which he knows he can trust, not serving his own ambition. It is hard to see how Shakespeare could have managed things better, for when France says,

> *Gods, gods! 'tis strange that from their cold'st neglect*
> *My love should kindle to inflam'd respect,*

we find ourselves answering, 'No, not really strange at all!'

If Cordelia's farewell to her sisters also has something of the metallic, the self-righteous and cheaply sarcastic about it ('The jewels of our father . . .'), we have to remember that she too has to learn, the only way we ever do, by suffering. Moreover, a cool and dignified speech at this juncture would sound false—complacent and insufficiently anxious—and Cordelia has to say something, for she will be absent from the scene for a long time to come. Rather amusingly, it is the bad sisters who insist on Cordelia's lovingness and loveableness (something we might not be altogether convinced of at this stage), when they allude to the 'poor judgment' with which their father has cast her off.

So ends what must be the weightiest, most packed, single scene in Shakespeare.

SCENE II

'Thou, Nature, art my goddess . . .' The historical
critics, quickly shuffling into their smelly doublets and
hose, have put Edmund in his place before he appears—
or just as soon as he appears. 'No medieval devil ever
bounced on the stage with a more scandalous self-
announcement', says John F. Danby.* This, I take it,
means that although Edmund speaks a lot of good modern
sense, we ought to feel obliged to ignore much of what he
says, and hence to discount the energy, the life, the ingenuity in him—which, alas, is all the more striking for
the poor show Edgar puts up much of the time. 'Now,
gods, stand up for bastards!' Perhaps they don't, as the
play turns out, or not less ambiguously than they stand
up for anyone else. But it seems to me that Shakespeare
stands up for this particular bastard, who has had an unlucky start in life: unlike Regan and Goneril, the women
who pull him down with their love as they pull their father
down with their lack of love. Scandalous? It is a splendid
speech, and all the history in the world won't persuade us
at this point that 'Nature' is such a reprehensible concept
by comparison with 'custom' or the mere 'curiosity of
nations'. Says Edmund, 'Fine word, "legitimate"!' We
are to suffer so many dreary fine words from his legitimate
brother.

Edmund's play-acting with the letter is nicely adapted
to the sort of man that Gloucester, as we have so far seen
him, appears to be.

> This villain of mine comes under the prediction; there's son
> against father: the King falls from bias of nature; there's father
> against child. We have seen the best of our time . . .

There is no need to dwell on the skilful, the seemingly
inevitable, interweaving of sub-plot with plot—which, one

* *Shakespeare's Doctrine of Nature*, 1949.

might ask, is which?—except to confess that finally one cannot really imagine the one without the other.

> Fut! I should have been that I am had the maidenliest star in the firmament twinkled on my bastardizing.

Edmund's discourse on 'the excellent foppery of the world' is modern good sense, and also medieval and indeed ancient good sense and good morality:

> An admirable evasion of whoremaster man, to lay his goatish disposition to the charge of a star!

We tell ourselves that, even so, it is the speech of a bad man, devoid of respect for authority, law and other higher things, a Machiavel, a Faust without a German university education behind him: we tell ourselves that the stars, the 'planetary influence', are here standing in for the God of Christianity, and it is a case of Shakespeare striving to be a pagan just as we, we are told, must strive to be Elizabethans. We may not convince ourselves entirely, or even be convinced by Coleridge's sensible reminder that 'scorn and misanthropy are often the anticipations and mouthpieces of wisdom in the detection of superstitions', and that one can fall below superstitions as well as rise above them. Our feeling of admiration for Edmund, however reluctant or anachronistic, is likely to be increased by the scant and feeble performance put on by Edgar immediately afterwards. 'Some villain hath done me wrong.' In the enjoyment of his trickery, Edmund is so bold as almost to give the show away: 'I am no honest man if there be any good meaning toward you.' The passage is a lively enactment of Edmund's contention that bastards are richer in 'composition and fierce quality', and it is just as well that Shakespeare reminds us, through Edmund, that Edgar is

> *a brother noble,*
> *Whose nature is so far from doing harms*
> *That he suspects none.*

SCENE III

Idle old man,
That still would manage those authorities
That he hath given away! Now, by my life,
Old fools are babes again . . .

Bradley's comment on Caesar's description of Antony as 'the old ruffian' fits this too: 'there is a horrid aptness in the phrase, but it disgusts us'. These true words are more detestable on Goneril's lips than are Edmund's true words on his lips. Whatever Gloucester may have given him in the way of 'breeding', Edmund owes a good deal less to his father than do these two daughters; he has to make his own way.

'His knights grow riotous . . .' Perhaps they do, but we don't see any signs of it.

The technique the daughters employ to rid themselves of the inconvenient father and the monarch not-quite-retired is as simple and crude as that used by a gang of children to drive away an unwanted outsider—and as effective. A hundred knights are reduced to fifty, fifty to five-and-twenty—they pass the ball one to the other over their victim's head, until the victim himself becomes the ball—then to ten, to five, to none at all. Then they go inside and lock their doors against him. It is not due to any poverty of imagination that their way of treating Lear is so obvious, so unsubtle: for crudeness is of the essence. Lear is not to be handled as an ex-monarch, unloved but feared, who poses certain problems of state by his continued presence on the scene. He is to be made to see himself as something much less grand than that—as a dirty, incontinent, drunken old fool, a domestic nuisance at a time when unhappily there was no geriatric ward to which he could be committed. Or as a dirty little boy, from a bad neighbourhood, who has a running nose and ringworm and probably other disgusting diseases. His humiliations are to be of the grossest sort; his tormentors are to be contemptuously casual, not diabolically ingenious; his higher education is to be of the most direct and most unsubtle kind. Indeed, so effective is the treatment they mete out to him that Kent's presence is needed as a reminder that Lear is not identical with the Lear 'image' created by the words and actions of his daughters:

LEAR. What would'st thou?

KENT. Service.

LEAR. Who would'st thou serve?

KENT. You.

LEAR. Dost thou know me, fellow?

KENT. No, Sir; but you have that in your countenance which I would fain call master.

LEAR. What's that?

KENT. Authority.

The most pitiful part of Lear's suffering is not his raving and rambling in the storm: this is beyond pity, unless (like Lamb) we pity him in the sense of wanting to take him in out of the storm. Perhaps Lamb was right, and these passages cannot be acted. What I have in mind can be, though; it is all eminently actable: what the sisters say and how they say it, and in especial Lear's painful efforts to persuade himself that things are not as bad as they seem, his forced attempts to look on a dimly perceived bright side. It is true that such attempts are in no way disinterested, since he is unwilling to acknowledge the fact that he has made a colossal misjudgment; his pride will for some time require him to believe, to try to believe, that he was not altogether wrong. But against that consideration we must place this other: that he is having to fight against his own nature; he is seeking, now in the face of real provocation, not to be rash, seeking to understand, to be patient and even to be sympathetic towards the failings of others.

This theme is announced in the present scene, when the Knight remarks that

> there's a great abatement of kindness appears as well in the general dependants as in the Duke himself also and your daughter,

and Lear replies,

> I have perceived a most faint neglect of late; which I have rather blamed as mine own jealous curiosity than as a very pretence and purpose of unkindness.

It is developed, after the 'repudiation' of Goneril, in Act II Scene iv, with Lear's reaction to the sight of Kent in the stocks:

> *They durst not do't,*
> *They could not, would not do't; 'tis worse than murther,*
> *To do upon respect such violent outrage.*
> *Resolve me, with all modest haste, which way*
> *Thou might'st deserve, or they impose, this usage,*
> *Coming from us.*

He would welcome an explanation which could justify 'this usage', though obviously he cannot conceive its nature! Then follows his rage when informed that Cornwall and Regan are weary after their journey and unable to see him. 'Mere fetches, ay, The images of revolt and flying off': he is right first time. 'The King would speak with Cornwall': now he is deceiving himself that he is still king; and that he is dear to Regan: 'the dear father Would with his daughter speak . . .' Then he attempts a more moving self-deception:

> *Tell the hot Duke that—*
> *No, but not yet; may be he is not well:*
> *Infirmity doth still neglect all office*
> *Whereto our health is bound; we are not ourselves*
> *When Nature, being oppress'd, commands the mind*

To suffer with the body. I'll forbear;
And am fall'n out with my more headier will,
To take the indispos'd and sickly fit
For the sound man.

For Lear as we have known him, this is a long speech to have as its theme extenuation of other people's weaknesses, quite a remarkable admission that even kings and fathers must be prepared to put up with a little neglect when their subjects and daughters are not feeling too well. The attempt at patience and understanding evaporates abruptly when his eyes fall on Kent, the King's man, not merely neglected, but imprisoned in the stocks. 'I would have all well betwixt you', says Gloucester pathetically, echoing Lear's forlorn hope.

The hope that all, or something at least, may still be well despite plain appearances revives briefly on the appearance of Regan: she *cannot* be as bad as Goneril, lightning doesn't strike twice in the same place, or not so violently. So poor Lear strives to differentiate between these two daughters: because Goneril is a vulture, a serpent, therefore Regan cannot but be 'tender-hefted' by comparison. Any man may be faced with the necessity of cursing one of his daughters, or even two, but not three, not that! The theme of attempted self-deception collapses when (enunciating the desperate theory that 'wicked creatures yet do look well-favour'd When others are more wicked') Lear doubles back on his tracks. Regan is insisting that he should keep only twenty-five knights, whereas Goneril was proposing to cut his train to fifty, and is therefore 'twice her love'. It is a horrible parody of bargaining in the bazaars, love has been reduced to arithmetic; and of course Lear is now getting the treatment which he dealt out to Cordelia, what L. C. Knights neatly describes as his 'habit of arithmetical computation of degrees of affection'.* At that time, the more words the

* *Some Shakespearean Themes,* 1959.

more love; at this time, the more followers the more love, or rather the less hatred and contempt. The Fool had told him in advance, in Act I Scene v, what the result of his computation would be: Regan will taste as like Goneril 'as a crab does to a crab'. There is nothing possible for Lear now, except to rush out into the storm.

ACT I SCENE IV

Retracing our footsteps, we perceive that at this stage Lear certainly hasn't got round to the idea that he is no longer king: 'Let me not stay a jot for dinner: go, get it ready.' He is quite sure of the next meal: 'if I like thee no worse after dinner I will not part from thee yet'. This remark to the disguised Kent is grimly amusing in retrospect, since Lear is not to part from Kent until he dies, and perhaps not even then.

Lear's first questioning of his identity takes the form of a fairly jocular threat, a casual joke from his own point of view: 'Who am I, sir?' Oswald replies very apropos, 'My Lady's father', and is immediately struck by Lear and tripped up by Kent. This is an easy little victory, and clearly there is work for the Fool to do, as the conscience of the king. Enough has been written about the Fool, and it will suffice here to suggest that his function is a double and paradoxical one, to needle Lear into a sharper consciousness of his folly and to remind him of Cordelia while this is necessary, and later on to try to distract him from the thought of his foolishness and (like sleep) to keep him alive for further suffering and sane for the sake of humility. In the latter stages one feels that the Fool's efforts are also bent towards keeping himself sane; he doesn't have the physical strength of Lear, Kent and Edgar, he is something of an effete intellectual, a critic of the times, and distinctly out of his class on the heath, the first to die (presumably) victim of Lear's obstinate pride. At the present time Lear is in need of reminding, not of distracting, and this is obviously a more dangerous job: 'Take heed, sirrah; the whip.' But this is also the Fool's heyday, for practically every character is legitimately the butt of his wit; he is indeed, or in one sense, 'all-licens'd'.

We notice that Lear's second questioning of his identity, falling very soon after the first, is considerably less light-hearted. 'Are you our daughter? . . . Does any here know me? This is not Lear . . . Ha! waking? 'tis not so. Who is it that can tell me who I am? . . . I would learn that . . . Your name, fair gentlewoman?' Even so, he still has, or thinks he has, 'left a daughter',

> *another daughter,*
> *Who, I am sure, is kind and comfortable:*
> *When she shall hear this of thee, with her nails*
> *She'll flay thy wolvish visage.*

He is right, of course, in that he still has or will have Cordelia: but it would not be Cordelia's style to flay with her nails Goneril's or anyone else's visage, however wolvish, and (a deeper irony) if it were in her nature to behave so, it probably wouldn't be in her nature to love her father still and to succour him at such risk to herself. Lear sees himself as the centre of the universe, and sees loyalty to himself as the sole measure of goodness or badness in others.

We note also the likeness to Lady Macbeth in Goneril's contemptuous remark flung at her husband concerning 'this milky gentleness and course of yours'. Though the relations between these two couples are so very different, Albany's reply, 'Striving to better, oft we mar what's well', may make us think of Macbeth's altogether more poignant words:

> *We will proceed no further in this business:*
> *He hath honour'd me of late; and I have bought*

Golden opinions from all sorts of people,
Which would be worn now in their newest gloss,
Not cast aside so soon.

ACT II SCENE I

Edmund's skilful stage-management increases our reluctant admiration for him, and also our sense of Edgar's
simplicity: 'Draw; seem to defend yourself; now quit you
well.' How easily this noble, honest youth falls in with the
openly less-than-honest proposals of his brother ('In cunning I must draw my sword upon you'). Relentlessly con-
scripting everything into her service, Regan of course
takes Edgar's apparent murderousness as further evidence of the undesirability of Lear's retinue:

> *Was he not companion with the riotous knights*
> *That tended upon my father?*

And Edmund rushes to agree: 'Yes, Madam, he was of
that consort.' A moment of grim amusement will occur in
Act II Scene v when Edmund has denounced his father to
Cornwall, and the latter (who has something of Regan's
sharpness of wit) remarks that in that case it was not
solely Edgar's evil disposition that led him to seek his
father's death!

SCENE II

Maynard Mack writes, 'Kent in the stocks brings us
back to that distinctive feature of *King Lear*: its com-
bination of parable and parable situations with acute
realism.'* It is the realism that matters. Realism, in the
hands of a poet (I suspect one could say, in the hands of
any writer of any account), inevitably tends towards parable.

* *King Lear in Our Time*, 1966.

C   33

Without realism there won't be any parable, and here the parable is of so fine a sort that we don't think to use the word of it.

SCENE III

Edgar's account of his intended disguise carries the first intimation we have that the realm of Britain doesn't consist solely of 'shadowy forests . . . champains . . . plenteous rivers and wide-skirted meads' and 'validity and pleasure'. It now appears that there are also low farms and poor pelting villages and Bedlam beggars, a part of his kingdom which Lear still has to acquaint himself with.

SCENE IV

After the cruel tossing back and forth between his daughters, there is nothing Lear can do but rush out into the approaching storm. But before doing so, he delivers a speech which is one of the finest in Shakespeare, fine in varying ways and in its varying:

> *O! reason not the need; our basest beggars*
> *Are in the poorest thing superfluous:*
> *Allow not nature more than nature needs,*
> *Man's life is cheap as beast's . . .*

At this stage he indicates that at least he is aware of 'our beggars', and to the point at which he is able to note that even the poorest of them possesses a little more than is strictly necessary to survival. He has not yet met Poor Tom. We need more than the basic necessities if we are not to live at the level of beasts; and one thing we need is love or affection.

The speech begins in reason (though an impassioned reasonableness), and it is a chastened king who is ready to argue by reference to beggars, even though he cannot resist a mild dig at his fashionably dressed daughters. The spark of malice quickly burns out, as tears, another habit of women, come to his eyes. Reasonableness too is extinguished, for anger is the best antidote to tears:

> *No, you unnatural hags,*
> *I will have such revenges on you both*
> *That all the world shall—I will do such things,*
> *What they are, yet I know not, but they shall be*
> *The terrors of the earth.*

This, too, is very like a bullied and helpless child: I'll get my own back on you, I haven't yet decided how, but . . . Lear, as a king, would know all about power and punishment, but he cannot deceive himself that he knows the shape of the 'things' he will do to his daughters: little by little he is having to realise his utter powerlessness. In the event he is to have his 'revenges', and shadowy enough they are, in Act III Scene vi, in the fantasy trial at which a madman and a Fool officiate as judges: 'It shall be done; I will arraign them straight.'

Once Lear has been provoked into rushing away, his daughters agree that they would gladly accommodate him; it is only his followers (even though reduced to one) that they object to.

ACT III SCENE I

> *This night, wherein the cub-drawn bear would couch,*
> *The lion and the belly-pinched wolf*
> *Keep their fur dry, unbonneted he runs,*
> *And bids what will take all.*

Students sometimes interpret Lear's words,

> *Allow not nature more than nature needs,*
> *Man's life is cheap as beast's,*

along with his comment on Poor Tom,

> thou art the thing itself; unaccommodated man is no more but
> such a poor, bare, forked animal as thou art,

as signifying that clothes make the man and that, bereft of such artificial aids to dignity, man is seen to be the same as the animals. The recurrent animal imagery in the play is then adduced to support this view as being the outcome of the play as a whole: at the best man is an unaccommodated animal, at the worst an animal accommodated with especially sharp fangs. But the function of the animal references is not to establish a fundamental likeness between man and animal, but rather to distinguish fundamentally between them. The shock that is generated at the sight of men doing what animals would not do, or of men treating men worse than they would treat the savagest and most hostile animals, is a recognition of the essential wrongness of the situation, not an acknowledgment of its essential truth:

> *If wolves had at thy gate howl'd that dearn time,*
> *Thou should'st have said 'Good porter, turn the key.'*

We should be clear in our minds that neither the storm (which no man ought to have to be out in) nor Tom's lack of 'accommodation' (which no man ought to suffer) actually turns men into animals. Lear doesn't turn into a wild beast, nor does Tom (though he makes a good madman) even seem to be a wild beast, or even a mild one like the worm Gloucester mentions in Act IV Scene ix—for one thing, he complains too much! The beasts are Goneril and Regan, who are not out in the storm, nor 'unaccommodated'. Lear has remarked on their fashionable attire: clothes obviously don't make the woman. But Lear's speech is a hard one: 'Is man no more than this?' We must recognise that the peculiar intensity of Lear's re-education has brought him near to madness, real madness, at this moment; that this particular Bedlam beggar *is* 'more than this' in a quite obvious sense; and that other persons are to show that not all men are 'no more than this', however unaccommodated with power they may be. Only the road of excess can lead Lear towards the palace of wisdom, and to his brief sojourn in it. Having believed that all men are his loving and reverent subjects, he must come to believe that all men are animals before he finds out that some are capable of unforced, indeed of self-jeopardising, love and reverence. To *know* this is a great thing, and, to quote Blake again,

> *Great things are done when men and mountains meet;*
> *This is not done by jostling in the street.*

SCENE II

Lear's strong propensity for self-regard, the continuance of his conscious 'kingliness', is well brought out in the earlier part of this scene. Where the crown used to reside is now 'my white head', 'a head So old and white as this', a fit—and perhaps the only really fit—target for thunderbolts. Kent and others point out that this storm is no ordinary one, but one fit for a king. If Lear is to die, then (according to Lear's way of looking at things) the whole world must die, man must come to an end:

> *And thou, all-shaking thunder,*
> *Strike flat the thick rotundity o' th' world!*
> *Crack Nature's moulds . . .*

More than usually, we welcome the Fool's practical common sense (what Maynard Mack calls his 'wry idiom, vehicle of the hard-won wisdom of the poor'), with its

plain implication that the lightning isn't likely to strike
Lear's daughters or their dwellings:

> O Nuncle, court holy-water in a dry house is better than this
> rain-water out o' door.

The self-dramatisation continues, however; and one feels
like telling Lear that, too true, there would be no point at
all in his taxing the elements with unkindness, and, true
too, they owe him no subscription, and it is well known
that the winter wind is not so unkind as man's ingratitude
and the bitter sky does not bite so nigh as benefits forgot.
At the same time, this behaviour of Lear is not entirely
illegitimate: he is a big man, and we see his greatness at
the same time as we see the need for him to be humbled:

> *here I stand, your slave,*
> *A poor, infirm, weak, and despis'd old man.*

In fact there is not much infirmity of that sort in evidence
at the moment, and the Fool's job here is to deflate, a little,
lest we should be tempted to pity or admire his master to
excess. The song about the cod-piece, which is otherwise
not especially relevant, will do this by virtue of its easy
vulgarity. The cod-piece is a great leveller.

Lear's succeeding speech (following on his resolution
to 'be the pattern of all patience' and 'say nothing') would
seem to mark a step forward since, though the injustice
done to him is not far below the surface of his mind, he is
talking of the fallibility of justice in general. The last
sentence, however, shows that he has far to go yet:

> *I am a man*
> *More sinn'd against than sinning.*

This is not yet indubitably true. If the line has any
significance at all for the play, it only derives from the
uncertain acknowledgment that he *has* sinned. Lear's self-
pity is alleviated by his touch of concern for the Fool immediately after:

I have one part in my heart
That's sorry yet for thee.

SCENE III

This brief passage marks the beginning of our admiration for Gloucester, who resolves to help the King 'if I die for it, as no less is threatened me', and the ending of our admiration for Edmund, who resolves to denounce his father to the Duke.

SCENE IV

The paradox whereby the Fool both augments Lear's anguish and palliates it is reflected in the paradox whereby Lear tells us first that the tempest in his mind renders him immune to the storm outside (only when the mind is free is the body delicate), and secondly, a few lines later, that the tempest outside distracts his attention from 'things would hurt me more'. It would not do for the storm really to take his mind off what he has done and what is being done to him, nor would it do for him to be truly oblivious, scantily accommodated as he is, to the storm as a physical reality capable of inflicting suffering and hardship on 'poor naked wretches' wheresoever they are.

He makes the Fool go into the hovel before him, as the weaker vessel—though, true, it is more fitting that the Fool should be scared by Poor Tom than the King—and then, for the first time, he really speaks of the miseries of others, about those who are worse off than he:

O! I have ta'en
Too little care of this. Take physic, Pomp;
Expose thyself to feel what wretches feel,
That thou mayst shake the superflux to them,
And show the Heavens more just.

The sentiment is to be echoed, as Kenneth Muir points out in the notes to the Arden edition, by Gloucester at a similar stage in his journey (Act IV Scene i):

> *Heavens, deal so still!*
> *Let the superfluous and lust-dieted man,*
> *That slaves your ordinance, that will not see*
> *Because he does not feel, feel your power quickly;*
> *So distribution should undo excess,*
> *And each man have enough.*

Shakespeare makes his point clearly enough: this personal suffering will come to nothing unless it is seen and feelingly recognised as a sharing of the common lot, and moreover as something for which the sufferer himself may have to bear a degree of responsibility. It was not the Gods who brought poverty into existence, they have nothing to do with it, but it is still up to men to save Heaven's face by contriving a just distribution of the world's goods.

H. A. Mason (whose response to Shakespeare is always fresh and vivid, though not always, some may feel, apt)* is scandalised that Lear should have managed to reach old age before realising what it is to be poor. 'I can only say,

---

* He seems to agree with John Middleton Murry (*Shakespeare* 1936) —though he is squeamish about actually saying so—that *Lear* is 'lacking in imaginative control' and 'the work of a Shakespeare who is out of his depth'. Mr. Mason admits that 'Some extraordinary arguments will have to be put forward before any sane reader will consent to share in a re-reading of the last two acts of *King Lear* which might have as a result a loss of satisfaction, a lower estimate of the play.' Well, some of us do get a kick out of that sort of masochism. But Mr Mason doesn't advance the requisitely extraordinary arguments; in fact he advances some fresh and persuasive appreciation of the play, including these two acts, which will require those arguments to be even more extraordinary in future. We feel all the more acutely, with Hazlitt, that 'if there is anything in any author like this . . . we are glad of it; but it is in some author that we have not read.' Incidentally, Murry remarked in the preface to a later edition of his book (1954) that his treatment of *Lear* was 'confessedly unsatisfactory' and 'it was preposterous in me to say that Shakespeare was out of his depth, when the evidence stares me in the face that I was out of mine.'

what appalling spiritual blindness he must have spent his life in, and a blindness hard to credit in the Middle Ages, when the physical and moral facts of poverty were evident to the lord who (by proxy) gave daily alms at his gate and had his duty dinned into him by his spiritual adviser. Poverty was not a tabooed subject then.'*

Perhaps we should do well to forget the Middle Ages—especially if we cannot remember them too clearly. In any age blindness is easily procured and maintained towards the distresses of others—which one then sees every day without really seeing. Spiritual advisers and an absence of taboo could as well lead to a greater insensitivity as to a greater sensitivity. For all their Christian advantages, I doubt whether the Middle Ages were very different in this respect from the present day in some parts of Asia, if not some parts of Europe. One can give one's conscience money to a beggar every day without coming to *know* what poverty is like. And even—or especially—if one is a king. I would say that Lear's reflections are, in the words of Joseph Warton, 'equally proper and striking'. It has been dinned into us by our own spiritual advisers, the critics, that this play is about blindness, but even so I do not believe we are meant to suppose that Lear has been *exceptionally* blind to poverty, or egregiously callous. In this respect, as in others, what he (by his loss) wins through to is not merely the ordinary knowledge or 'sight' which other people have had all along, but something much deeper and keener. The play isn't simply 'corrective' on the level of a humours comedy.

'O, what a world's convention of agonies is here!' said Coleridge. 'All external nature in a storm, all moral nature convulsed,—the real madness of Lear, the feigned madness of Edgar, the babbling of the Fool, the desperate fidelity of Kent.' Much has been written on the mad

* '*King Lear*: Manipulating Our Sympathies', *The Cambridge Quarterly*, Vol. II No. 2, 1967.

scenes, not all of it so much to the point as this. Students with a taste for such grand encapsulations as 'the reversal of the natural order' are quick to tell you that these scenes show how in a bad world good men must disguise themselves in order to survive, and the disguises serve to emphasise the badness. We hardly need to have the badness of this world rubbed in! Besides what peripheral significances they may have, these scenes are *crucial*, I would say.

In his misery Lear still sees himself as a king, unique and isolated in his experiences, still the nonpareil, a Niobe or a *pater dolorosus* in reverse. His pride is essentially undiminished, and he is still the centre of the universe, though now it is an utterly different universe, and he is a dragon of sorrow instead of a dragon of wrath. These scenes are necessary to persuade him that others suffer in much the same way, sometimes more acutely, sometimes undeservedly, that suffering (unlike ruling) is not the prerogative of kings. He must be brought to see himself as a commoner in Rilke's Land of Pain; the storm in external nature and the convention in the hovel enable him to recognise his kin. The essential declaration, the words which mark if not the crossing of the frontier then certainly the arrival at it, are 'I have ta'en Too little care of this', words which are to be related to both Lear the ruler and Lear the private person. These words are spoken before the first appearance to him of Poor Tom, but Lear's recognition must be enforced and confirmed. If Lear is not brought to this settled recognition, this acknowledgment that he is but one among many, then he will take Cordelia's sacrifice as a matter of course, as an expected tribute to his greatness—instead of what it is, a sign of *her* greatness.

The movement of the play is intricate, and the play's cogency is bound up with its following a course which is not the shortest distance between two fixed points. Lear is in the borderland between sanity and madness, and to treat us to formal speeches announcing a change of heart would obviously be disastrous. While forced to grant that other people can be reduced to misery, he is self-obsessed to the point of assuming that it must be their daughters who have so reduced them, and thus his first utterance on the appearance of Poor Tom is

> *Didst thou give all to thy daughters?*
> *And art thou come to this?*

his second is identical,

> *What! has his daughters brought him to this pass?*
> *Couldst thou save nothing? Would'st thou give 'em all?*

and his third is an extension of his curse on his own daughters to include Tom's:

> *Now all the plagues that in the pendulous air*
> *Hang fated o'er men's faults light on thy daughters!*

As Kent tries to point out, Tom/Edgar has no daughters; the irony is that while Lear equates Tom's situation with his own, in truth Edgar's situation is rather to be equated with Cordelia's. At the present moment, that is to say.

As regards the crucial significance I have described above, it does not matter that Tom is *not* a beggar but a young nobleman in temporary difficulties; he is readily accepted by the play's figures and audience alike as a representative of the Bedlam beggars of whom the country gives him 'proof and precedent'. Tom serves Lear well. Whether he serves Edgar well is another matter. For Edgar plays the part with what seems an excessive zest, or doggedness. It is as if he were trapped inside his disguise, unable to reveal himself, or simply unwilling to. Yet he could hardly be afraid of being denounced in this company! Perhaps it was Shakespeare's awareness of the unfavourable impression Edgar is making that led him to insert that aside in Act III Scene vi:

> *My tears begin to take his part so much,*
> *They mar my counterfeiting.*

43

Though Kent still preserves his disguise—for (we feel not a shadow of a doubt) utterly unselfish reasons—we cannot imagine him playing the lunatic at this juncture. And Edgar is such a dreary and heartless moraliser, with a pronounced inclination to priggishness. At the end of this same desolate scene he treats us to a disquisition on the well-worn theme of how suffering is more easily borne when one suffers in company. Kenneth Muir defends the soliloquy on the grounds that it is necessary to bring out the parallelism between the two plots, but this could be done (where in fact it is done) in the half-line, 'He childed as I father'd!' The rest of the passage prompts us to the suspicion that Shakespeare didn't write it; even these five words prompt us to the thought that Edgar is rather more preoccupied with his own sorrows than the *jeune premier* properly ought to be, despite his own comment (with which we agree too swiftly) that his pain seems 'light and portable' compared with the distresses of Lear.

Much more inept is his outbreak of moralising at the sight of his father, blinded and cast out, in Act iv Scene i:

> *World, world, O world!*
> *But that thy strange mutations make us hate thee,*
> *Life would not yield to age.*

That's to say, Gloucester must be thus ill-treated so that in due course Edgar will be prepared to accept old age and death! These lines, incidentally, follow those in which he consoles himself that

> *The lamentable change is from the best;*
> *The worst returns to laughter,*

and which are very like Rosse's cheery words to Lady Macduff a few minutes before she is murdered:

> *Things at the worst will cease, or else climb upward*
> *To what they were before.*

44

A cold-blooded son indeed, he stands aside and mumbles to himself,

> *O Gods! Who is't can say 'I am at the worst'?*
> *I am worse than e'er I was,*

as if he cannot bear to break off his fascinating train of thought, and then,

> *And worse I may be yet; the worst is not*
> *So long as we can say 'This is the worst.'*

The feebleness of these self-regarding deliberations is the more clearly exposed by their occurrence in the interstices of some fine speeches from Gloucester, the truly cogent moralising of

> *I have no way, and therefore want no eyes;*
> *I stumbled when I saw. Full oft 'tis seen,*
> *Our means secure us, and our mere defects*
> *Prove our commodities,*

and the true pathos of

> *I' th' last night's storm I such a fellow saw,*
> *Which made me think a man a worm. My son*
> *Came then into my mind; and yet my mind*
> *Was then scarce friends with him. I have heard*
> *more since . . .*

Edgar's aside, 'How should this be?', in whatever way we interpret it, cannot but be damagingly inapposite. Bad indeed is the trade that must play the fool to sorrow, angering itself and others! Why does Edgar persist in it?

Even less admirable is his celebrated résumé of his father's career in Act v Scene iii:

> *The Gods are just, and of our pleasant vices*
> *Make instruments to plague us;*
> *The dark and vicious place where thee he got*
> *Cost him his eyes.*

This is stylistically a cut above his other animadversions, technically a very neat piece of work (the dark place, the deed of darkness, the darkness of blindness), and its style almost deters us from examining its content. H. A. Mason is right in calling it 'cheap' and in bringing to our attention the fact that what cost Gloucester his eyes was his humane feelings of now, not his lechery of years ago.* Yet Professor Muir claims that Edgar's epigram is 'the dramatic answer to Gloucester's cry' in Act iv Scene i,

As flies to wanton boys, are we to th' Gods;
They kill us for their sport.

It is more a counter-assertion than an answer. And Gloucester's punishment is judicious indeed, as per the copybook maxim, Be sure your sins will find you out! But it is strange to see academics who desire to make a neatly Christian work out of this play advancing so barbaric an argument. Old Testament morality, perhaps—an eye for an eye—but scarcely Christian, one would have thought. Perhaps they would be even better pleased if Gloucester were to be stoned to death as well as blinded. In his son these sentiments sound even worse than in a high-minded professor.† We wonder a little that Edgar should eventu-

* 'No doubt I should instantly be challenged to name one other eccentric beside myself if I said that *we* have been longing for somebody to wring Edgar's neck.' ('*King Lear*: Radical Incoherence?', *The Cambridge Quarterly*, Vol. II No. 3, 1967). Mr Mason is welcome to name me.

† William Empson writes thus: '. . . even the resentful Edgar and the sex-resenting Shakespeare cannot have believed all through the play that Gloucester deserved to have his eyes put out; the sort of justice imputed to the gods is what is called "poetic", happening through agencies which have obviously no real sense of justice. And the way the gods do it is by "plaguing" us, and by inventing "instruments", that is, instruments of torture; they are also facetious and full of mean jeering tricks.' (*The Structure of Complex Words*, 1951). We cannot see in Edgar a son so unnatural as to have believed 'all through the play' that his father deserved to be blinded because of an old 'pleasant vice': on the contrary, he utters not a word of complaint or reproach. The accident of the blinding merely serves to switch on his moralising mechanism, and he talks about his father as if he were someone in an old tale. But neither can we believe for a moment that Edgar himself sees the justice he is talking about as 'poetic' in Professor Empson's sense (viz., aesthetically pleasing, otherwise revolting). If only we could!

ally confess that his therapy was mistaken—'Never—O fault!—reveal'd myself unto him'—if that is what he is doing, since quite possibly Gloucester's death is also included in this divine wish for revenge. Unhappily for his standing in our eyes, Edgar is going to gain by it.

Returning to Act III Scene iv, and the first appearance of Tom, we note that he lowers the tone of the discourse pretty promptly:

> one that slept in the contriving of lust, and wak'd to do it. Wine lov'd I deeply, dice dearly, and in woman out-paramour'd the Turk ... Let not the creaking of shoes nor the rustling of silks betray thy poor heart to woman: keep thy foot out of brothels, thy hand out of plackets ...

No doubt lust, his father's, *could* be said to have undone Edgar. And the Fool, himself a somewhat frail, virginal little figure, is licensed to make jokes, and many jokes are of a sexual nature: 'This is a brave night to cool a courtezan', and so forth. But what are we to make of Lear's outburst of sexual disgust in Act IV Scene vi?—

> *Behold yond simp'ring dame,*
> *Whose face between her forks presages snow;*
> *That minces virtue, and does shake the head*
> *To hear of pleasure's name;*
> *The fitchew nor the soiled horse goes to't*
> *With a more riotous appetite.*
> *Down from the waist they are Centaurs,*
> *Though women all above:*
> *But to the girdle do the Gods inherit,*
> *Beneath is all the fiend's: there's hell, there's*
>   *darkness,*
> *There is the sulphurous pit—burning, scalding,*
> *Stench, consumption ...*

Professor Muir's remarks that 'as the Elizabethans knew, certain kinds of madness are accompanied by such

an obsession' and 'sexual desire has led to the birth of
unnatural children' do not account for the intensity of this
loathing. Apart from Gloucester's ancient lapse, the question of sexual lust or female unchastity has not arisen in
the play. It can be argued, of course, that the speech looks
forward to the lust-triangle formed by the two daughters
and Edmund, an intrigue in which the women make the
running and the man is more hunted than hunter; and it
is true that Goneril and Regan are women—but so is
Cordelia, whom at this stage Lear is refusing to see because
'a sovereign shame so elbows him'; and Lear himself was
born of woman and of sexual desire. My own feeling is
that the speech will have to be taken as just one mani-
festation of Lear's madness, otherwise gratuitous, except
possibly as a reminder that the by-products of suffering,
however regenerative that suffering may ultimately be,
are not always very seemly. The outburst certainly encourages those readers who consider that Edgar's effect
has been to drive Lear more rapidly into insanity! But the
important thing, in any case, is not Lear's insanity, or
whether or how he falls or is driven into it, but the condition of mind in which he re-emerges from it: his final
sanity.

SCENE VI

Of Lear's 'revenges' upon his daughters, in the form
of a fantasy trial, Ronald Peacock has remarked, 'At the
moment of greatest breakdown we are given a judgment
that represents amidst chaos the memory of civilization.'*
It is a faint and ambiguous memory then, for the 'trial'
gets no further than bare accusation—Goneril 'kick'd the
poor King her father', while Regan has 'warp'd looks' and

* *The Poet in the Theatre,* 1946.

a hard heart—and thereupon the fantasy-Regan or perhaps Goneril escapes: 'Stop her there! . . . Corruption in
the place!' The sentence,

> *To have a thousand with red burning spits*
> *Come hizzing in upon 'em,*

precedes the hearing, and no judgment is delivered. The
fantasy breaks down, Lear is not to be allowed to escape
from reality so soon, and the tired old man falls asleep, a
merciful respite if you like, but also a prolonger of life
and therefore of suffering.

The Fool speaks his last words: 'And I'll go to bed at
noon.' He doesn't survive to see Cordelia again. Lear's
words in his own last speech, 'And my poor fool is
hang'd!', must refer primarily to Cordelia. The term is
one of endearment, though it could bear its modern meaning too, for Albany has just been declaiming with peculiar
insensitivity his intention to see that

> *All friends shall taste*
> *The wages of their virtue, and all foes*
> *The cup of their deservings,*

and Cordelia is the kind of altruistic and imprudent 'fool'
whose virtue is rewarded with death. Lear can well be
referring to the Fool as well, though secondarily and at
some remove, for he has been a sort of substitute-Cordelia
for Lear, though inevitably an inadequate one, and as
Bradley points out, it is the Fool to whom Lear turns in
Act II Scene iv: 'O Fool! I shall go mad.' The Fool is the
most feminine of Lear's companions, indeed a good deal
frailer than Cordelia, and the thought of him might recur
to Lear at this point by the sort of confusion between his
two affectionate dependants which has been suggested by
Bradley and William Empson.

SCENE VII

> *I am tied to th' stake, and I must stand the*
> *course.*

The extreme courage and dignity with which Gloucester behaves in this confrontation with Cornwall and
Regan goes a long way to cast into grave doubt his son
Edgar's favourite theory that 'the Gods are just'. He
might seem to have suggested his own fate when he says
he sent the king to Dover

> *Because I would not see thy cruel nails*
> *Pluck out his poor old eyes,*

and of course when he says

> *I shall see*
> *The winged vengeance overtake such children,*

except that Goneril had the idea at the beginning of the
scene. The incident of the servant (a shade of Kent) who
intervenes to try to save his second eye, while it serves the
needs of the plot, does more than that: for one thing, we
can do with a reminder of humanity at this point; for
another, it demonstrates Regan's 'manliness', for she
seizes a sword and attacks the servant from behind. The
play on the word 'see' is repeated, and the other eye is put
out. We should also observe that Gloucester is exceedingly
prompt to acknowledge his error about his sons: 'O my
follies! Then Edgar was abus'd': he has already travelled
a long way from the smug old fuddy-duddy of the play's
opening. The genuineness of Shakespeare's interest in the
'sub-plot' is evidenced in the following scene, Act iv
Scene i, where, as I have remarked, Gloucester has some
splendid things to say. He grows rapidly in stature. We
should also remark his thoughtfulness towards the Old

Man, who is an innocent where he, he knows, is less than innocent,

> *Away, get thee away; good friend, be gone:*
> *Thy comforts can do me no good at all;*
> *Thee they may hurt,*

and also towards Tom: 'bring some covering for this naked soul'.*

The word-play on 'seeing' is sustained by Gloucester now, in 'I stumbled when I saw' and in

> *Oh! dear son Edgar,*
> *The food of thy abused father's wrath;*
> *Might I but live to see thee in my touch,*
> *I'd say I had eyes again.*

That Edgar can manage to refrain from declaring himself to his father, that he can stay paralysed in his banal and egotistical little moralisings, argues a staggering lack of natural feeling (the contrast with Cordelia is sharp), or else a notable excess of British phlegm! But no doubt there will be critics to argue that Edgar, like his gods, is just. Bradley remarks that he is 'the most religious person in the play'. If this is true, it is extra evidence that the play is not religious in any sense of the word that springs to mind.

ACT IV SCENE II

Albany's rehabilitation at this stage—he has taken a long time to discover that the wrong side has been turned out—is not altogether credible, but this is a minor point. Where the question of 'justice' is concerned, the scene offers a very interesting epitome of the situation. The newly emergent Albany has declared that if the heavens

* Mr. Mason has a fine passage on Gloucester's goodness of soul in 'King Lear: Manipulating Our Sympathies'.

are not seen to punish these offenders quickly, then men
will turn into cannibals, 'like monsters of the deep'. Then
'Enter a Messenger' to report that the Duke of Cornwall
is dead, slain in an act of villainy (though at the cost of one
good man, the servant, killed too). Albany cries,

> *This shows you are above,*
> *You justicers, that these our nether crimes*
> *So speedily can venge!*

His next words are,

> *But, O poor Gloucester!*
> *Lost he his other eye?*

And the answer comes, 'Both, both, my Lord.' This
'justice' falls on the good and on the bad alike.

SCENE III

> *You have seen*
> *Sunshine and rain at once; her smiles and tears*
> *Were like, a better way; those happy smilets*
> *That play'd on her ripe lip seem'd not to know*
> *What guests were in her eyes . . .*

The celebrated description of Cordelia reading the letters
anticipates the divided state of mind at death of Gloucester, whose heart

> *'Twixt two extremes of passion, joy and grief,*
> *Burst smilingly,*

and of Lear,

> *Do you see this? Look on her, look, her lips,*
> *Look there, look there!*

This is the true condition of tragedy, an ambiguousness
which is yet far from mere paradox, and (if I may labour
the point) even further from a simple recognition of justice

having been done. To say this is not to suggest that tragedy is something very grand, remote, exotic or esoteric, but rather the contrary: that here art is at its remotest from the fairy-tale and at its nearest to the common realities of life.

The account of Lear's partial emergence into sanity, because it has been so well prepared for, can be related instead of enacted—especially when Shakespeare is relating it:

> *A sovereign shame so elbows him: his own unkindness,*
> *That stripp'd her from his benediction, turn'd her*
> *To foreign casualties, gave her dear rights*
> *To his dog-hearted daughters, these things sting*
> *His mind so venomously that burning shame*
> *Detains him from Cordelia.*

The effect of these lines is intensified in that it is Kent who speaks them. This is the shame of a king, and the shame is kingly, all-mastering, it has brought its subject to his knees, almost.

SCENE IV

It is good, to put it mildly, to have Cordelia back. She has retained a vivid, even specialist, intimacy with the various weeds that grow in the sustaining corn of her native land. There is a sad irony in her remark, apropos of her father's 'bereaved sense', that 'He that helps him take all my outward worth', since she, the only one who can truly help him, is to lose all her outward worth thereby.

Her words at the end of this scene,

> *No blown ambition doth our arms incite,*
> *But love, dear love, and our ag'd father's right,*

though we grasp the precautionary significance of them, have an oddly and displeasingly operatic ring about them, a prima-donnaish quality which is altogether alien to the speaker. No doubt the critic is right in pointing out this sort of thing; though I have never myself perceived there was any pressing need to encourage people to sneer at literature. Shakespeare's defects, anyway, would be the high points of—but there is no call to mention names.

SCENE VI

> *O you mighty Gods!*
> *This world I do renounce, and in your sights*
> *Shake patiently my great affliction off . . .*

Gloucester's grounds for suicide are that, if he lives any longer, he is going to quarrel, uselessly and impiously, with the 'opposeless wills' of the Gods. He is not entirely logical here, since if it is the will of the Gods that you should die, you will die without any effort on your part, but we can go along with Kenneth Muir's note, to the effect that rebellion against the Gods is to be thought of as a worse sin than suicide. Logically, Edgar's therapy ought to work: as he points out, it is a 'miracle' that Gloucester still lives after his supposed fall from the cliff, that is to say, his survival was willed by the Gods:

> *Think that the clearest Gods, who make them honours*
> *Of men's impossibilities, have preserved thee.*

Gloucester (and I believe in this he represents the tendency of the play as a whole) doesn't confirm Edgar's high-flown sentiments about the Gods and their 'honours', indeed he doesn't mention the Gods at all. His answer is short and simple:

> *henceforth I'll bear*
> *Affliction till it do cry out itself*
> *'Enough, enough,' and die.*

This is a truer modesty of spirit, which leads one neither to rebel against whatever gods may be nor to hurry to declare oneself of their party. We feel a greater respect for Gloucester than we would if he joined in the pious moralisings of his lay-preacher son. These moralisings are discredited by the appearance as if on cue of Lear 'fantastically dressed with wild flowers'. Edgar's first reaction—

> *But who comes here?*
> *The safer sense will ne'er accommodate*
> *His master thus*

—could only be excused if there were any danger of the audience supposing that the King was on his way home from a nearby carnival of flowers. His second reaction is more apt—'O thou side-piercing sight!'—for it is a sight calculated to deflate Edgar's Pippa-like philosophising.

Lear's ramblings are of course much to the point. A Canute who has learnt a harder way, he is applying his newly gained wisdom to the past:

> They flattered me like a dog, and told me I had the white hairs in my beard ere the black ones were there. To say 'ay' and 'no' to every thing that I said! 'Ay' and 'no' too was no good divinity. When the rain came to wet me once and the wind to make me chatter, when the thunder would not peace at my bidding, there I found 'em, there I smelt 'em out. Go to, they are not men o' their words: they told me I was every thing; 'tis a lie, I am not ague-proof.

It is fitting, too, that while in the process of humility, of recognition of his limitations ('they told me I was every thing'), Lear should momentarily remind himself and us that he was, even so, a great man and a king: 'Ay, every inch a king . . .' That 'a dog's obey'd in office' does not signify that Authority is always a dog. It is not the intention of the play that he should collapse into *abjection*, which would be merely a form of evasion, an inverted arrogance. The amazing thing is that, far from being a muddle, the scene shows us so much of Lear's sanity as well as his insanity, and that a state of soul is expounded in the course of what seems the portrayal of a state of mindlessness.

Again Shakespeare feels it necessary to tell us that Edgar's heart is breaking, lest we should conclude he has none. It was perhaps the playwright's distrust of his audience, rather than of Edgar, which prompted him to put these words in the latter's mouth:

> *O! matter and impertinency mix'd;*
> *Reason in madness.*

Latterly, apart from 'yond simp'ring dame' and so forth, there has been much more reason than madness in Lear's outbursts. This is no mere madman, it is *Lear* mad. It is possible that Shakespeare never did anything more awe-inspiring, more impossible-seeming, than this—to take a petulant old retired monarch, drive him mad and stick flowers in his hair, and still end with a figure of tragedy.

In a very slightly ambiguous passage,

> *You ever-gentle Gods, take my breath from me:*
> *Let not my worser spirit tempt me again*
> *To die before you please!*

Gloucester indicates his resolve not to take his life, a senti-ment which gratifies the still-disguised Edgar: 'Well pray you, father.' But immediately afterwards he declares him-self quite willing that Oswald's 'friendly hand' should do the job for him, and a little later he wishes somewhat un-regenerately that he were mad like the King and thus not conscious of his woes. He is not altogether reconciled to those opposeless wills.

Cordelia has changed too. She has grown up, she talks and behaves like a queen. The perfect courtesy of her bearing towards Kent says much for the King of France, and for the rightness of his intuition in taking her for his wife. It also says a lot for her courage and love that she should ever return to this barbarous Britain.

The Doctor, a prime example of his profession, wants Cordelia to be near when Lear wakes: 'I doubt not of his temperance.' And true, when Lear wakes, he is 'temperate', he thinks he is in hell (where else could he temperately expect to be?) and he recognises the face of Cordelia as that of 'a soul in bliss', or one that is destined for heaven. The living Cordelia, he must suppose, would never come near him, so 'You are a spirit, I know; where did you die?' Cordelia murmurs, 'Still, still, far wide', but he is not, he is feeling his way closer, in the only way that is right for him. He has recognised her as Cordelia, but he cannot bring himself to declare his recognition until he is 'assur'd Of my condition', and until he has knelt to her, and only then at the end of a tentative, apologetic, hesitant speech in which he acknowledges with an aptly humble indirectness that he has no right to expect her to be there, to assume publicly that she is there, even if he is privately sure that she is:

> *Do not laugh at me;*
> *For, as I am a man, I think this lady*
> *To be my child Cordelia.*

Only when she has assured him that she *is* his child Cordelia, does he feel able to express his penitence in words— few but very sane, very much and directly to the point: 'If you have poison for me, I will drink it.' Shakespeare's cognisance of when *not* to have speeches, as in the discovery of Hermione to Leontes, is evinced here in the sparseness and simplicity of the words spoken by Cordelia. We see—and the sight throws light back upon the 'contest' out of which the play has grown—that she is still averse to wordy protestations of love:

And so I am, I am.

And,

No cause, no cause.

And thereafter,

Will't please your Highness walk?

We readily understand that loquaciousness would be out of place in a person such as Cordelia, yet even so there cannot be many persons whether in Shakespeare or elsewhere who attain to such greatness of presence and yet utter so few words. But then, so many other persons (including, paradoxically, her sisters) have spoken for her throughout the play's unfolding that she has never really been away. As Bradley says, this is a scene 'which it seems almost a profanity to touch'.

ACT V SCENE I

No doubt it is proper in Albany to be 'full of alteration And self-reproving', as Edmund (that quiet, efficient operator) puts it. It is also proper that we should merely be told briefly about this and not shown it. It is something a lesser dramatist would have made more of.

Regan's exploratory remarks to Edmund concerning his relations with her sister are peculiarly repellent in their wording; a minor point though this is, it casts its little cloud of doubt on the theory that Shakespeare was out of his depth in this play. Edmund, it seems, has been rather too efficient:

> *To both these sisters have I sworn my love;*
> *Each jealous of the other, as the stung*
> *Are of the adder. Which of them shall I take?*
> *Both? one? or neither? Neither can be enjoy'd*
> *If both remain alive . . .*

Edmund is unable to answer his question at the moment, but he acknowledges the answer, with superbly wry wit, when it dawns upon him in Scene iii.

SCENE II

Finding that Lear and Cordelia have been taken prisoner, Edgar is not quite able to bring out his pious philosophy of the Gods and their justness, but instructs his father (who understandably doesn't see the point of trudging any further) that 'ripeness is all'. This seems to me to signify not so much that we should be ready for death as that we shouldn't seek to anticipate it. Gloucester could make out a strong case for his own ripeness for death. It is death's readiness for us which is the issue, I would think, not our readiness for it. And perhaps this is the justification for Edgar's flight and his long-sustained disguise.

Too far gone for moralising, Gloucester has placed himself passively in the hands of his son, and the normal father-son relationship is thus reversed, but quite normally so, considering their ages and physical conditions, and it proves nothing apart from Edgar's filial love and Gloucester's debility.

SCENE III

> *We are not the first*
> *Who, with best meaning, have incurr'd the worst,*

says Cordelia, older than her years, too old to share
Edgar's complacent views on justice. And, incidentally,
doesn't one line from her count for more than a lucu-
bratory page from Edgar? She is speaking of her past (her
meaning was good during the love-competition) as well as
of her present—and, alas, of her future. *King Lear* can
hardly be 'summed up', but Cordelia's simple words seem
to me to stand very near to the heart of the play.

The succeeding speech by Lear beggars description
and makes commentary look foolish. The pattern of their
brief future is laid down in the lines,

> *When thou dost ask me blessing, I'll kneel down,*
> *And ask of thee forgiveness . . .*

and it was prefigured in Act IV Scene vii, when Lear awoke
and desired to kneel, whereas Cordelia desired him to
'hold your hand in benediction o'er me'. Both are to be
satisfied now, she receiving his blessing while he receives
her forgiveness, their loves interlock and they are not to
be separated again. It has been a long journey from 'Nothing, my lord' and 'Nothing will come of nothing' to this.

> *Whatever dies, was not mix'd equally;*
> *If our two loves be one, or, thou and I*
> *Love so alike, that none do slacken,*
> > *none can die. . .*

So firm and certain is their relationship, the world of their
tested and proved love, that they can laugh at 'gilded
butterflies', whether literal butterflies at liberty or metaphorical butterflies imprisoned in court life, and amuse

themselves with speculating about 'who's in, who's out', confident that behind the iron bars which make no prison for them, they will

> *wear out*
> . . . *packs and sects of great ones*
> *That ebb and flow by th' moon.*

Though Lear's prognosis is incorrect, his diagnosis is accurate—and this is what matters.

> *Upon such sacrifices, my Cordelia,*
> *The Gods themselves throw incense.*

I cannot agree with those who believe that what is meant by 'such sacrifices' is the renunciation of the world by Lear and Cordelia. For one thing, the new Lear is certainly not going to credit himself with making any sacrifice whatsoever; and for another, and lesser, he hasn't renounced the world, he has simply been made prisoner and the world has been taken away from him. The sacrifices—certainly any sacrifices Lear can talk about—are all Cordelia's, and it is on those and on her that the Gods will throw incense, or ought to.

'Wipe thine eyes.' Lear is in no fit state to be a king again, but he is a man again, with somebody to protect. Cordelia is courageous, but she is not merely humouring him by pretending to be a frightened little girl; she knows what to expect from her sisters, and she has never deluded herself about consequences.

Edmund makes a good end in the second part of the scene, as good as anyone can who has just arranged for the murder of Lear and Cordelia. He assents to Edgar's famous and infamous epigram about the Gods being just, perhaps because he is dying, in the way Gloucester agreed because he was enfeebled. At the best of times it would be a waste of labour to argue with so pertinacious and assured a moralist. Edgar's account of what he has been up to all this time savours unpleasantly of selfishness—how *he* was persecuted, how *he* suffered—as well as tedious and gratuitous moralising:

> *O! our lives' sweetness,*
> *That we the pain of death would hourly die*
> *Rather than die at once!*

In extenuation we may plead that he is young, that he has been learning the hard way (though not so hard a way as Lear), and that he feels obliged to repeat his lessons aloud. Had he not felt called upon to recount the longish story about Kent falling into a trance ('List a brief tale . . .'), Lear and Cordelia might have been saved, we tell ourselves, bitterly and of course foolishly. But all the more for Edgar's verbosity do we find ourselves admiring the succinctness of Edmund's epigram, which could never come from a superficial nature, let alone a mere stage Machiavel:

> *I was contracted to them both: all three*
> *Now marry in an instant.*

Albany too is afflicted with the justice tic, remarking of the deaths of Regan and Goneril that

> *This judgment of the heavens, that makes us tremble,*
> *Touches us not with pity.**

A moment later, the most sheerly terrible thing in English drama, Lear enters with Cordelia dead in his arms. If this too is a judgment of the heavens, then indeed we can only tremble! The only judgment that it makes the bystanders think of is the Last Judgment, or rather that collapse of

---

* He is wrong. In tracing the theme of personal love and loyalty in the play, Arthur Sewell quotes the lines,

> *Yet Edmund was belov'd:*
> *The one the other poison'd for my sake,*
> *And after slew herself,*

and adds, pertinently I think, 'The weeds, after all, spring from the same soil as the "sustaining corn".' (*Character and Society in Shakespeare*, 1951.)

everything, indiscriminately, which shall precede judgment:*

KENT. *Is this the promis'd end?*
EDG. *Or image of that horror?*
ALB. *Fall and cease.*

Lear is a man again. Though he has failed to save Cordelia, he has killed the hangman, and this access of strength is of course not merely the last spasm of a mad, dying, old man or some other well-known medical phenomenon, but the direct product and measure of his love. We feel the poignancy of his reference to the softness of Cordelia's voice, 'gentle and low, an excellent thing in woman', once (as he reckoned) all too soft and low.

'All's cheerless, dark, and deadly', says Kent. But not to the spectator of this finest of all works of tragedy. The new Albany must show his briskness and start to make administrative provisions for the future, until he notices that the old King is dying. The young and insensitive Edgar tries to revive Lear—a good touch, this—while the older and wiser Kent prays that his heart will break: 'Vex not his ghost: O! let him pass . . .' For a moment we ourselves are afraid that Lear will not die.

Professor Muir quotes Bradley, inaccurately, as believing that Lear dies of joy, in the belief that Cordelia is alive. What he dies of, of course, is exhaustion—'the wonder is he hath endur'd so long'—but it seems that he dies *in* joy, allowed to believe at the last moment that Cordelia is alive, a minute mercy which none the less seems to us of considerable moment.

Or is this a wrong, a sentimental reading? Must Lear die in full knowledge that Cordelia is dead? I think not, I

* The theme of the end of the world has been sounded twice before, in Lear's first speech on the heath ('Crack Nature's moulds, all germens spill at once That makes ingrateful man!') and, as Kenneth Muir points out, in Gloucester's recognition of Lear in Act IV Scene iv ('O ruin'd piece of Nature! This great world Shall so wear out to naught').

think we do not need to deprive him of that final mercy which nature quite often shows men at the last. 'Mine eyes are not o' th' best': but it is not (I would say) a sign of senility or self-deception in him that he should think she lives, but rather it is a sign of the strength (even at this moment) of his love for her. He *wants* her to be alive, he doesn't give up hope (even *we* don't want her to die!), he would tear her back from death if he could: this surely is the 'impassion'd clay' that Keats spoke of. At *this* point it is right that Lear should resist the truth. Without this, his parting from Cordelia would seem abrupt, a little cold, resigned, almost casual. But finally, having had one's say, one feels inclined to agree with Bradley, that 'to dwell on the pathos of Lear's last speech would be an impertinence'.

We are glad that the faithful Kent, only doubtfully acknowledged by Lear as his servant Caius, is granted a fine couplet as he withdraws from the triumvirate or duumvirate proposed by Albany:

> *I have a journey, sir, shortly to go;*
> *My master calls me, I must not say no.*

All the actors on the heath must die, Lear and Kent and the Fool, all except the indefatigable Edgar, who drops the curtain aptly on the play with a brief tribute to the old and a reminder to himself that he is young and 'shall never see so much, nor live so long'. The events of the last few minutes must have gone some way towards rubbing off his priggishness and discouraging his readiness to moralise. He ought to make quite an efficient ruler.

*   *   *

I recall a student's essay which ended thus: 'Good does indeed triumph in the end, and the wicked die a deserved death . . . Gloucester dies, Lear dies, Cordelia dies, Kent dies, the Fool dies.' In that Johnson could see no justice in

Cordelia's death, his shocked response was right. It was his expectations that were wrong. Not his expectations of life ('a play in which the wicked prosper, and the virtuous miscarry, may doubtless be good, because it is a just representation of the common events of human life'), but his expectations of art ('all reasonable beings naturally love justice' and 'it is always a writer's duty to make the world better'). Johnson's attitude is easier to account for than that of some modern critics who are far too sophisticated to imagine that art is necessarily a fairy tale hopefully intended to make the world a better place to live in, and yet contrive to find that, at the end of *Lear*, justice—some peculiarly rarefied and oblique form of it—somehow triumphs!

Professor Wilson Knight has remarked that 'these gods are, in fact, man-made'. And each man makes his own, out of his own need, urgent or casual. Against the varying statements concerning the Gods and justice (and the variation cannot be simply and solely attributed to the different characters who make these statements and the differing circumstances in which they are made)—against this confused cloud of witnesses stand, in striking contrast, the repeated and consistent statements about endurance, patience, courage, fortitude.* Here the play speaks with a single and firm voice. The wicked are punished; or rather, since evil is their good, they punish themselves: the way in which Edmund and the two sisters come to ruin is altogether reasonable and realistic. Apart from that, justice is not done. Man does without it. Man does without the Gods; at the most, having created them in the image of his own virtues or vices, he derives some slight comfort from appealing to his own creations in times of crisis, of defeat or triumph. Edmund, that villain, was right, except that he misconceived the nature of his own

* See Kenneth Muir, Introduction to the Arden edition of *Lear*, pp. lxi–lxii.

God or Goddess, Nature. Men live, and sometimes live well—and die well—in the absence of justice.

By lacking the intervention of just gods, men indicate what justice is or would be—as Cordelia, intent on securing justice for her father, incurs the unmistakable injustice of a common hanging, what Professor Wilson Knight calls 'the most hideous and degrading' of all deaths—but their greatness is that they do not yield to what they consider evil or give up the fight even while knowing that virtue can only be its own reward: they are themselves 'just', just to the best that is in them. The play is about men and life. We may hope that the Gods would indeed throw incense on Cordelia's sacrifices, but we may also suspect that, should it be brought to their notice, they would be likely to send down fire upon this book of Shakespeare's. *Lear* makes our 'tough-minded' modern plays, those niggling studies in 'absurdity' and hopelessness and gratuitous violence, look what they are—lifeless scribblings on a small-town lavatory wall.

'ANTONY AND CLEOPATRA'

Nobody is Perfect

'ANTONY AND CLEOPATRA'
NOBODY IS PERFECT

THE teacher revises his valuation as also his understanding of a work of literature in the act of teaching it. If he finds that his views are growing more firmly defined by a process of reaction against the prevalent views of his pupils, this does not mean that they are necessarily false or falsely arrived at. In any case I have always felt a considerable admiration for *Antony and Cleopatra*. In earlier times my admiration was a trifle shame-faced, for it was, I recognised, in some part an infatuation for Cleopatra as the super-*femme-fatale* of a proleptic super-cinema. Having for the past several years had to contend with the sharp and only too spontaneous disapproval of both heroine and hero evinced by business-like Singaporean students—a case no doubt of 'youth restraining reckless middle age'—I find my admiration for the play growing less shame-faced.

For these young people Antony emerges as 'a dirty old man', Cleopatra as 'an ageing prostitute who has already had many lovers', and the Egyptians are seen as a gang of Levantine layabouts. Cleopatra sometimes receives a certain grudging respect (she is after all a wily near-Oriental, fighting in her own way on her home ground), but poor Antony, colonial officer, is observed to fail in everything he turns his hand to: 'he cannot even succeed in killing himself'. In the new countries politics are all—all for politics, and the world well gained—and a man who jeopardises his position as the triple pillar of the world for the sake of a woman will be despised by the young women even more thoroughly, it seems, than by the young men. At the same time, perhaps because an ancient feeling persists that success in politics requires some unseemly sacrifice of the saintly virtues and even of the humane ones, I have never encountered any really warm admiration for Octavius Caesar. He is seen to be, as A. C. Bradley saw him, 'very formidable': neither less nor more.

It does not seem probable that many academics, either, are fitted by nature or experience to find the play moving, or not in any way other than the detachedly moralistic. Cleopatra in turn has few qualities to fit her for domestic life in an academic community. (In extenuation of this cheap gibe I can only plead the sad exasperation set up by the spectacle of grown men dismissing Cleopatra as a help-meet for themselves without asking themselves what share they have of Antony in their composition.) And so, what with the hard-headed young and the cool-hearted old, *Antony and Cleopatra* is a play doomed to be underestimated of late, and it is indeed a striking tribute to its 'poetry' that for the sake of its poetry it has not been relegated below the second class of Shakespeare's productions.

In this essay I shall have frequent reference to H. A. Mason's lengthy study of the play.* To venture that the play which Mr. Mason is describing should be called *Antony, Cleopatra and Mr. Mason*, while it indicates a sense of slight obtrusiveness on the critic's part, is chiefly meant as a tribute to a critic who has really involved himself in the work of art, humanly, face to face, without benefit of metaphysics. The complaints listed in the introduction certainly do not apply to Mr. Mason, who is so scrupulous and therefore 'minute' as to risk that effect of occasional ludicrousness which I know I have achieved regularly throughout this book. At the same time, and I think it is as well to state this plainly now, I cannot accept the distinction which Mr. Mason draws, 'comparable to that we

* *The Cambridge Quarterly*, Vol. I Nos. 3 and 4, 1966.

make in life when contrasting deeds with words', between 'spell-binding' poetry and 'the manacling power of true drama'. In inferior dramatists poetry often goes counter to the moral drift, for instance in Massinger's *A New Way to Pay Old Debts* where Sir Giles Overreach gets all there is of the former, or in Webster and Tourneur, where the poetry sticks out like a sore thumb, or rather a superior sort of lollipop. But Shakespeare is not an inferior dramatist, and *Antony and Cleopatra* is patently one of his major works, and written more than sporadically in poetry. In lesser dramatists, when 'poetry' pulls one way and 'drama' another, then 'drama' loses—while the 'poetry' at least gains a place in dictionaries of quotations. In the case of *Antony and Cleopatra* either the 'spell-binding' is part of the 'manacling power of true drama', or else it is not truly spell-binding. Or else, of course, the play is not a true drama: which I cannot believe.

* * *

ACT I SCENE I

Mr. Mason finds what he calls 'juggling' right at the beginning, in a rather unexpected context—unexpected because most critics are ready to allow Antony to have been an unreservedly great soldier before Cleopatra got her hooks into him:

> *those his goodly eyes,*
> *That o'er the files and musters of the war*
> *Have glow'd like plated Mars . . .*

'Grammatically, it is true, his eyes are merely *compared* to the god in armour,' says Mr. Mason, 'but the god-like fire passes back and would turn Antony at the very least into a demi-god of war . . . as soon as it could combine with the right dramatic material.' But surely this is just soldier's talk, one sort of soldier's talk, spoken by a person described as 'a friend of Antony', one who does precious little for his friend? At a comparable juncture Macbeth was described as 'Bellona's bridegroom', whereas in fact he was Lady Macbeth's. It is necessary that Antony should be recognised as a great general, or a formerly great general, and the comparison with Mars is the obvious one to make, all too obvious. The succeeding lines,

> *his captain's heart,*
> *Which in the scuffles of great fights hath burst*
> *The buckles on his breast,*

are 'good dramatic poetry', according to Mr. Mason, where the earlier lines are merely 'good poetry', because they are validated by the course of the action of the play. One's conception of the course of action will, however, be affected by one's judgment of these passages as they present themselves, though it may not be affected very much. And my own opinion is that the earlier lines are not particularly good 'poetry' (but conventional soldier's lingo) and the later lines are not especially good 'dramatic poetry' (but an obvious lead-in to the soldier's conventional view of women, one which is to be much more cogently and yet much more equivocally stated by Enobarbus).

This second passage is almost as hyperbolical as the first, for it pictures Antony as a professional strong-man, bursting out of his breast-plate like a circus performer. Then Philo goes on to complain that instead of continuing to wreck his armour, Antony's heart has renounced all *moderation* and changed into a bellows and a fan to cool a gipsy's lust. Antony is seen as serving Cleopatra's lust: and what Philo and his colleagues object to is the idea of a woman using a man, and not (which is in the natural order of things) a man making use of a woman. The theory (not Mr. Mason's, I hasten to say) which has it that the

72

soldiers in this play are the truly objective judges of Cleopatra, that they are the author's mouthpiece for uttering what *he* thinks of this woman, strikes me as utterly ridiculous. For these soldiers, women are essentially camp followers, and the camp doesn't follow *them*; they are there to be used and disposed of, and Antony's crime is that he took a native girl too seriously and it affected his generalship. The most we can say of the soldiers' view of Cleopatra is that it is a soldier's view: we recognise its worldly wisdom, but if we suppose that it is also the limit of Shakespeare's wisdom, then the play is over before it has begun. The thought occurs to me, incidentally, that we literary people are not always wholly scrupulous in our dealings with the comparative processes. Thus the shade of Cleopatra, we say, moves through *The Waste Land*, majestic, vital and passionate, putting to shame the debilitated or squalid 'modern' women of the poem. Then we turn to Shakespeare's play and the reality from which this impressive shade derives, and we say that in reality there is little about this Egyptian woman that is truly majestic or unequivocally vital and passionate.

It also seems to me that the brief interchange between Antony and Cleopatra which follows is eminently normal. Mr. Mason's adduction of a passage from Stendhal to the effect that men who talk about their love prove thereby that they are not in love is beside the point: Shakespeare is not Stendhal (though the latter did talk quite a lot about love himself), and this play is not set in the French nineteenth century. Mr. Mason could as well have brought up Restoration comedy, or even a characteristic modern novel, where fornication is freely talked about, but rarely love. Antony's remark that 'There's beggary in the love that can be reckon'd' is not notably highflown or stupid. We may wish that it had occurred to Cordelia to make this point! But, more pertinently, why cannot these lovers be allowed their moments of affectionate badinage? Why is it

73

that critics are always pressing towards extremes, so that one party sees the essence of romantic love where the other sees falsehood, rhetoric and strain?

That 'Cleopatra's taunts reveal a head free from romantic nonsense and respect for Antony', as Mr. Mason puts it, is true—as long as the adjective 'romantic' in its pejorative sense is taken to apply to the second noun as well, and as long as one recognises the precise limitation set upon the taunting. Indeed the realisation of all this is essential to one's understanding of the play. This man and woman are past the age for 'romance', just as they are past the age when it is embarrassing to talk about love. That this is so helps to define the nature of the love between them, not to prove that love doesn't exist between them. The implication of the objections brought by some critics is that there is only one sort of love possible between man and woman, and this is the sort we witness in the case of Romeo and Juliet. (But more on that topic later.)

Certainly Cleopatra is teasing, or even taunting, Antony. This doesn't reduce their relationship to the level of a fumble in the back seats of a cinema or even in the corridors of power. If Cleopatra were a 'harmless household dove', then she wouldn't be an 'enchanting queen'; and perhaps it is a 'romantic' notion to suppose that a queen in love is likely to behave and feel in quite the same way as the maid that milks and does the meanest chores. We must allow a queen to be queenly, as queenly (at this very moment she reminds us that she is 'Egypt's queen') as is compatible with being in love. Yet some of us manage to accuse her in almost the same breath of being insufficiently a queen (a ruler with civic responsibilities) and insufficiently a good housewife. I can sympathise with the Indian playwright who, with the *Ramayana* in mind, recently insisted that in the modern theatre love should be made modern: 'it must not be the love of kings and nobles, but love that grips the common man, love of a peasant working

74

in the fields for his spouse, who brings him the midday meal, or the love of a factory hand for a co-worker'.* It is a sign of Shakespeare's inclusiveness, or perhaps one should rather say his sense of essentials, that he presents Antony and Cleopatra as queen and triumvir in love and also as common man and common woman in love. We are not used to such collocations, it might seem, we would prefer Shakespeare to have been simpler, more simple-minded or more single-minded. And possibly we do not like to see him engaging in full drive in a project which we have decided in advance is unsuitable by virtue of its subject-matter. We are almost of a party with those affronted students who believe that love is a condition which occurs in people only up to the age of twenty-five or below, or, if it obtains thereafter, bears a strong resemblance to I. A. Richards's Phantom Aesthetic State and neither affects nor is affected by anything other than the participants' bank accounts.

Of the speech, 'Let Rome in Tiber melt . . .', Mr. Mason comments that Antony is covering up 'his unawareness of the realities of his situation whether political, moral or amorous by giving us a specimen of the grand nonsense he can spout'. The realities of Antony's situation are many, and in some case mutually irreconcilable, and we can hardly expect him to reveal his cognisance of all of them in his every utterance. The present speech is directed by his awareness of one of the realities, his love for Cleopatra. That there is an element of rhetoric in it is true, for it is not Rome that is going to melt, it is Antony's followers, some of them, who are going to discandy. And it is also true that Cleopatra dissociates herself from her lover's hyperboles:

> *Excellent falsehood!*
> *Why did he marry Fulvia, and not love her?*
> *I'll seem the fool I am not . . .*

* *Writing in India*, edited by Nissim Ezekiel, 1965.

This is the superficial, defensive 'scepticism' of women in love, perhaps their form of an amulet against the evil eye: they want to believe what the man says, indeed they would be distressed if he didn't say it, but they take refuge in a semi-serious joke about the way he says it. This is shrewd psychology on Shakespeare's part, and essentially *normal* psychology.

Granted the element of rhetoric, do we really find the speech as a whole 'grand nonsense' and evidence that Antony is making an ass of himself and 'merely garlanding his ass's head with flowers'?

> *Kingdoms are clay: our dungy earth alike*
> *Feeds beast as man; the nobleness of life*
> *Is to do thus . . .*

This has a resonance about it (taken up by Cleopatra's much later lines about 'the dung, The beggar's nurse and Caesar's') which removes it far from any ass's head. To admit that later on Antony may now and again blush furiously to remember what he says here is only to grant that the course of true love, even middle-aged love, doesn't always run smooth, and at times won't for a time seem to be *true* love. Faced with the quite legitimate complexities of such a relationship, it is vain for us to wish that they were not so complex.

Considering Mr. Mason's interpretation of the scene, it is evidence of a fine scrupulosity in him that he should say, of the closing words of Demetrius—

> *I am full sorry*
> *That he approves the common liar, who*
> *Thus speaks of him at Rome . . .*

—that 'we are perhaps given a hint that the Romans may not be fit to pass a final judgment'. Demetrius is stating that the 'common liar', representative of the mob, the many-headed monster, the sweaty nightcaps, is actually right about Antony, for once at one with such superior persons as Demetrius and Philo. But we wonder whether this common liar can *ever* be right, entirely right.

SCENE II

Given a few of those good lines which overflow from Shakespeare's largesse, the soothsayer sounds like one of this author's dignified doctors whose modesty is so intimidating:

> *In nature's infinite book of secrecy*
> *A little I can read.*

His austerity and the equivocalness of his predictions bring out by contrast the Egyptian fecundity and cheerful grossness, here manifested in a jocular aspect:

> Let me be married to three kings in a forenoon, and widow them all: let me have a child at fifty, to whom Herod of Jewry may do homage . . .

No doubt Shakespeare didn't think about it, and probably we don't either, but this scene is a skilled mixture of the Elizabethan ('Prithee tell her but a worky-day fortune') and the Egyptian ('the o'erflowing Nilus', 'Isis', and—though this belongs to both categories—'Herod of Jewry'). John Dover Wilson has remarked of the local references that though they are 'all the merest commonplace', yet the sense of Egypt thus achieved is more convincing 'than any Egyptologist could have compassed with a lifetime of study behind him'.*

> *Rail thou in Fulvia's phrase, and taunt my faults*
> *With such full license, as both truth and malice*
> *Have power to utter . . .*

* Introduction, New Cambridge edition, 1950.

77

These words, in Antony's address to the messenger, seem to refer back to 'the common liar, who Thus speaks of him at Rome': it is peculiarly galling to have to grant that there is truth in accusations which are prompted by malice rather than by love of truth. It is part of the unhappiness of Antony's position that he cannot reject as solely malicious lying the charges which so many people bring against both him and Cleopatra.

Enobarbus shows himself at once an agreeable character, of whom one hopes for more. As Mr. Mason points out, his wit is elegant (at least until he remembers that he is a Roman soldier), and his amusing ironies do not register heavily as testimony against Cleopatra. His answer to Antony's drearily conventional wish that he had never seen her might even seem to suggest, light-hearted though the tone is, that once in Egypt Antony was doomed to end by love.

SCENE III

What this scene chiefly provides is a very apt performance on the part of 'the other woman'. Cleopatra exhibits jealousy of the legal wife, 'the married woman', and then brings up the old reproach that since her lover has been untrue to his wife, it is all too likely that he will be untrue to his mistress as well. These stock sentiments (and if she were deprived of them, Cleopatra wouldn't be a woman) are followed by something less ordinary, though still womanlike in trend if godlike in language:

> *Eternity was in our lips, and eyes,*
> *Bliss in our brows' bent; none our parts so poor,*
> *But was a race of heaven.*

And then by the defiant affirmation, 'They are so still . . .' Cleopatra's speeches at this point seem to me a nice, very human mixture of romantic love (large gestures and fine language) and unromantic suspicions and nagging. There is something of both these kinds of love, or both these ingredients of love, in the exclamation, 'Can Fulvia die?', another of Shakespeare's simple, reverberating, little phrases, and perhaps also in 'O most false love!' Antony of course doesn't come off anything like as well, but that is in the nature of things. He is by no means as adept in love-talk, and Cleopatra interrupts him when he is launched upon his soldier's talk. It is as if Donne's wife kept butting in as the poet was trying to deliver his valediction forbidding mourning. That, to quote Mr. Mason, 'nothing is clear' in this scene is of the scene's essence. It is a rather painful, edgy interchange: 'the toils are about them both: after this scene we cannot go on with any simple account of their relation'.

So far I am in agreement with Mr. Mason, but thereafter we part company. For Mr. Mason remarks, 'I try to enter into the action, but I am kept at a distance, forced to be merely a watcher, a reporter with an almost empty notebook.' I do not myself feel barred from the action, though I am conscious that the course of the action is far from straight. It is not Shakespeare's aim to make the relationship between the two seem simpler, even at this early stage, than he has conceived it as being. If he had done so, then I think we *would* be justified in feeling cheated later on! The almost-emptiness of the reporter's notebook is to be ascribed to the intended perplexedness of the proceedings, and not to their poverty. We are gathering information very quickly, but we cannot yet (and I think we never will be able to) reduce the proceedings to a résumé which shall be both neat and just.

SCENE IV

'Our great competitor' (Caesar's competitor or Caesar's *and* Lepidus's?)

> *fishes, drinks and wastes*
> *The lamps of night in revel,*

is unmanly and consorts with a woman who is unwomanly, tumbles on somebody else's bed, gives kingdoms away for a joke, drinks in company with the lower classes, reels through the midday streets, and leaves the hard work to his partners. While the particular charges are true, they range from the grave to the trivial (what is wrong with fishing?), from what concerns Caesar and presumably Lepidus to what concerns Antony alone, and the cumulative effect of Caesar's denunciation (though it is too judicial, or too cold, for this to be an apt description) is one of ludicrousness. Caesar is saying that what is wrong with Antony is simply everything: where Donne's lovers are every good thing and the poet of 'A Nocturnal upon St. Lucy's Day' is every dead thing, Antony is every bad thing, 'the abstract of all faults That all men follow'. We are far from being convinced that 'It is not Caesar's natural vice to hate Our great competitor', and, while neatly prognosticating the fate of Lepidus, the scene leaves us sceptical about the chances of any real *rapprochement* between the other two, whatever the concessions made by either or by both. There is still something apposite in Cassius's summing-up of them before the battle at Philippi: 'a peevish schoolboy . . . Join'd with a masquer and a reveller'.

I don't think our scepticism is modified much by Caesar's evocation, on receipt of the bad news about Menecrates and Menas, of the good old Antony, the tough soldier, defeated outside Modena, pursued by famine, yet patient in adversity and setting a wonderful example to his troops, as Plutarch reports. On that occasion Caesar was ranged against Antony, so he is now praising fortitude in someone whom he helped to vanquish, which is never a very difficult thing to do. It may be worth mentioning as an indication of the dislike Antony is able to arouse in some modern breasts, that I have seen this passage concerning the defeat at Modena and the consequent scarcity of food adduced as evidence that Antony's record as a soldier wasn't all that bright either! It is possible to be more grudging than Octavius Caesar.

Mr. Mason compares the scene with that in *Macbeth* (Act IV Scene iii) 'where the function also seems to be to provide the standards we need when we try to assess the faults of a man "in an imperial charge" '. Lust, that is, is comparatively harmless ('summer-seeming') in itself, but 'boundless intemperance In nature is a tyranny'. It wouldn't matter if Antony just had himself a good time with the woman—perhaps an Indian summer-seeming?— but alas he 'reneges all temper' and doesn't know when to stop. If this is the case, then either 'morals' don't come into the case at all or else the moral situation is a good deal less simple and straightforward than many critics have supposed it to be. But surely (though I believe the moral situation *is* less than especially simple) this scene is markedly different from that in *Macbeth*. We find Macduff more persuasive than Caesar because we have come to respect him and we know he is no contender himself for an empire, he is in that sense disinterested. Even so, I would not think of him as other than a somewhat ambiguous setter of standards! He shows himself prepared to be extremely indulgent towards Macbeth's potential successor since *almost* anything is going to be better than Macbeth. His standards are very 'special'.

All the way from Rome to Alexandria. And now we
have love described, remembered, day-dreamt; and even
testified to by a eunuch, who has fierce affections none the
less and thinks of what Venus did with Mars. The contrast with the preceding scene could hardly be sharper:
from 'the abstract of all faults That all men follow' we
move to 'my man of men', 'the demi-Atlas of this earth,
the arm And burgonet of men', from the unwomanly
'queen of Ptolemy' to 'great Egypt'. Of the lines,

> *He's speaking now,*
> *Or murmuring, 'Where's my serpent of old Nile?'*
> *For so he calls me,*

Hazlitt comments, 'how fine to make Cleopatra have this
consciousness of her own character . . .'

Shakespeare is not facing us with a choice of views, requiring us to accept one finally and reject the other out-
right. Antony and Cleopatra move between the two
extremes advanced in these two scenes, touching each
extreme at times, but not resting for long at either. The
problem the reporter will have with his notebook is that
either its pages will be left blank in the end or else they
will be scribbled all over illegibly!

Cleopatra has been imagining what Antony is doing at
that moment—perhaps he is on his horse. Then Alexas,
his messenger, arrives, with an account of how Antony
when he last saw him was in fact on a horse:

> *'Good friend,' quoth he,*
> *'Say the firm Roman to great Egypt sends*
> *This treasure of an oyster; at whose foot*
> *To mend the petty present, I will piece*
> *Her opulent throne with kingdoms. All the east,*

(Say thou) shall call her mistress.' So he nodded
And soberly did mount an arm-gaunt steed,
Which neigh'd so high, that what I would have spoke
Was beastly dumb'd by him.

Alexas's description, reminiscent of some boring canvas
painted by a specialist in battle-scenes or Great Men on
Horseback, is slightly comical; it certainly has little of the
natural persuasiveness of Cleopatra's preceding speculations:

Stands he, or sits he?
Or does he walk? or is he on his horse?
O happy horse to bear the weight of Antony!

The last line (if we take it along with the 'amorous
pinches' which Cleopatra is led on to think of) is possibly
a fleeting sexual memory, too tender and amused (though
we grant that Stendhal's ladies mightn't have mentioned
such a thing in public) to be called an innuendo, I hope.
Lascivious wassails, indeed! At all events, Cleopatra's
horse is of a rather different colour from Alexas's 'arm-
gaunt steed'.

The fishwife element, as evinced in her threat (how
serious?) to give Charmian bloody teeth for praising Julius
Caesar, is expunged from the impression this scene leaves
us with by the altogether captivating reference to her
'salad days'—one in the teeth for those priggish young
students! We feel with Mr. Mason, when he asks of the
scene, 'Is there one expression here we wish away?'

ACT II SCENE I

The second act opens rather curiously with a formal
though brief discussion of the gods and their justness.
Either these pirates are more philosophical than we may
have expected, or else, when Shakespeare has nothing

better for them to do, he sets his persons talking about divine justice. But Pompey quickly gets down to business, and to a more popular and proverbial idiom, and the scene livens up. He is less than chivalrous in his references to Cleopatra—since she is ageing, she will need more than her beauty to hold a man, she will need witchcraft as well —and his view of the couple is identical with Caesar's, while of course for his own immediate purposes he hopes their relationship will continue 'cloyless'. His passage on Epicurean cooks (a follow-up to Caesar's recent reference to the stale of horses and the bark of trees) makes one wonder whether his mouth isn't watering. In which case the news that Varrius brings of Antony on the move will dry it up smartly. Pompey's remark that Antony's soldier-ship is 'twice the other twain' ought to have precluded any misunderstanding derived from the Modena incident, and also the notion which some students form that Antony has been a notorious military wreck for years and what we are now to witness is the last wrigglings of a worm long chopped up.

The scene ends with another brief, brisk and eminently soldierly allusion to the gods. Let the outcome be as the gods will have it: we will do our best to see that the outcome favours us.

Having overheard Pompey and his friends on the state of affairs between Antony and Caesar, we now observe the meeting between these two: and a clever scene it is. The two big proud men circle each other like leaders of rival street gangs, while Lepidus plays the role of a nervous social worker. Antony's

> *I learn, you take things ill which are not so:*
> *Or being, concern you not*

84

could well refer to Caesar's strong feelings about fishing, public drunkenness, etc. The verbal fencing at times approaches the Miltonic manner in its deliberately unnatural phrasing:

> *So much uncurbable, her garboils, Caesar,*
> *Made out of her impatience, which not wanted*
> *Shrewdness of policy too, I grieving grant*
> *Did you too much disquiet: for that you must*
> *But say, I could not help it.*

Self-extenuation is not to interfere in the least with dignity, frankness and tact are to lie down together, and the olive branch is somehow to be offered and accepted without anyone being seen to handle it. Enobarbus chimes in like a voice from another world (or like the Fool in *Lear:* 'Truth's a dog must to kennel'):

> if you borrow one another's love for the instant, you may, when you hear no more words of Pompey, return it again: you shall have time to wrangle in, when you have nothing else to do.

This is refreshing in itself; and of course in a nicely plain way (in certain contexts plainness is a form of subtlety) it underlines the precariousness of the reconciliation when Antony rushes to silence his friend, 'a soldier only', not a politician.

The great men bustle out and the scene is transformed. Perhaps it is because this lowering exhibition of high politics has disgusted them that the soldiers, the lower ranks, now show themselves much less censorious towards the 'most triumphant lady' back in Alexandria. Enobarbus's description of her in her barge is not only sumptuous, it is also, in keen contrast to the prickly interchanges which have gone before, an impressively relaxed ('natural', one wants to say) piece of writing. Though Mr. Mason admires and apparently accepts F. R. Leavis' observation that the verse here 'seems to enact its meaning, to do and to give rather than to talk about',* he maintains that the verse does *too much*—it carries him 'both out of reality and out of the play and out of the company of the three men on the stage'. He complains that we are bound to feel the love-sick winds 'really were more than what the meteorologists might tell us': I don't know what the word 'really' is intended to signify here, but what is true (and surely unexceptionable) is that this is poetry and not meteorology. D. A. Traversi (who is elsewhere at great pains to be fair in his dealings with the play) has complained similarly that the beauty conveyed in this description is 'deliberately over-ripe, artificially opulent in its effect', and he takes special exception to the fact that the sails are purple, since 'the colour itself is, in a boat, unnatural'.† But this is neither a man-of-war nor a punt on the River Cam, and purple is a royal colour and specifically a Roman one: Cleopatra is flaunting the imperial colours in Antony's face! The winds are not love-sick *tout court*, it is worth noting, but love-sick for or on account of the sails which embrace them; the perfume of the sails may have an enervating effect on the winds, but luckily there are oarsmen in attendance and these are aided by an amorously following tide. So perhaps after all this is not an unfair description of a day on the river with little wind but a favourable current.

Mr. Mason asks whether it is 'possible to imagine the goddess in the barge hopping through the public street'. Perfectly possible, I would say, even without our imagination being assisted by extraneous information we may have gathered regarding the more than human mobility of some goddesses. Nothing more than imagination will be required, and not so awfully much of that. We have already heard enough about Cleopatra's versatility ('wrangling queen! Whom every thing becomes . . .'), and seen

* '*Antony and Cleopatra* and *All for Love*: A Critical Exercise', *Scrutiny*, Vol. V No. 2, 1936. † *Approach to Shakespeare*, 1938.

enough, for the transition Enobarbus makes from queen in royal barge to wench hopping through public street to be readily acceptable. And he has made the transition smoother by his gloss on her seemingly unseemly behaviour:

> *she did make defect perfection,*
> *And, breathless, power breathe forth.*

This *is* Cleopatra.

Mr. Mason's contention that 'we feel ourselves in a world where fancy has out-worked Nature' raises a complex question. Not as regards the barge itself, which is legitimately 'fancy', like any state procession or Lord Mayor's coach or, come to that, the Royal Barge of the King of Siam—and presumably Plutarch wasn't trying to bluff *his* readers—but as concerns Cleopatra and what she is. What is mere fancy in her, or whim, or affectation, and what is nature? There are times when one begins to feel, with Bradley, that the lecture platform is hardly the place for an enquiry of this degree of intimacy—and cold print is little better. And isn't this sense of a risked invasion of privacy in itself witness to the woman's reality, for unreality could never embarrass us so? I can only say that I find her more of a piece, for all her variety, than some readers do. 'Fancy' is a word we employ to describe something we disapprove of in another person; our use of the word won't prove, though, that whatever we are discussing is not natural, does not arise out of that person's nature. Nature or fancy? Some cases, perhaps, are clear enough: Cleopatra's is not, and we may call her a borderline case; in that, I suspect, she belongs to a majority rather than a minority.

But what we have here, in these passages, is not a contrast between nature or reality on the one hand and fancy on the other—a contrast which, having himself proposed it, Mr. Mason complains hasn't occurred to Enobarbus—but a contrast between two realities. If Enobarbus presents

them successively and not as explicit contrast, not as form-
ing a proposition likely to meet with objection or incredulity, it is simply because he sees them as equally true
of the one woman, the one (though 'rare') Egyptian. The
two aspects of Cleopatra are 'enacted' and not merely
talked about, and the scene says so much, so persuasively,
about her, that it is perverse to claim that what it says
cannot be reconciled with what is said about her elsewhere, earlier or later. If anything should have to go, we
must feel, it would not be *this*! J. I. M. Stewart has
summed up the situation well: 'In Cleopatra hidden
depths move and declare themselves; that these could not
be there is an arbitrary culture-assertion; that they are
there the poetry witnesses.'*

Incidentally, the lines,

> *Antony,*
> *Enthron'd i' the market-place, did sit alone,*
> *Whistling to the air; which, but for vacancy,*
> *Had gone to gaze on Cleopatra too,*
> *And made a gap in nature,*

in which Mr. Mason sees 'the supreme moment of fancy
that closes the passage', have always struck me as com-
prising a moment of wit rather than fancy (Enobarbus
returning to his proverbial style of talking), not glorifying
Cleopatra so much as poking fun at Antony, the visiting
V.I.P. from Rome, and serving to fend off any feeling we
might have developed that all this is (what Mr. Mason
calls it) a 'purple passage'. The lines about the market-
place provide a touch of dryness as the rather sweet wine
goes down. They also point towards Cleopatra's final
ascendancy over Antony, not as a bad human woman, but
as a truly remarkable Shakespearean creation: if he is rare,
she is rarer: that he is left with air to breathe on this

---

* *Character and Motive in Shakespeare*, 1949.

occasion is solely due to the law whereby nature abhors a vacuum.*

Enobarbus's judgment, his sense of reality, is certainly not impugned by his reply, at the end of the scene, to Maecenas's pious comment that now Antony must leave Cleopatra utterly: 'Never; he will not . . .' After what Enobarbus has just related concerning Cleopatra's infinite variety, Maecenas's brief catalogue of dry abstractions ('beauty, wisdom, modesty') can only point forward to the utter desertion of Octavia.

SCENE III

Bradley affirms that Antony 'brings himself to leave Cleopatra only because he knows he will return'.† We perceive that his self-deception as regards the possibility of remaining with Octavia certainly hasn't lasted long. The soothsayer's report on Caesar's 'natural luck' and the intimidation in his vicinity of Antony's spirit gives him a good 'reason' for running back to Egypt. Caesar beats him at dice, at tossing a coin, at cock-fighting! Of course we realise that, more importantly, 'i' the east my pleasure lies', and this pleasure is stronger than 'peace'. Unlucky at cards, lucky in love.

SCENE V

In Alexandria, with music, billiards, fishing. . . . These pastimes yield to reminiscing over Antony:

> *and next morn,*
> *Ere the ninth hour, I drunk him to his bed;*
> *Then put my tires and mantles on him, whilst*
> *I wore his sword Philippan.*

---

* Plutarch is a good deal more 'fanciful' and carries us further out of 'reality': ' . . . and there went a rumour in the people's mouths, that the goddess Venus was come to play with the god Bacchus, for the general good of all Asia'. † *Oxford Lectures on Poetry*, 1909.

This of course reminds us of that masculine queen and effeminate hero, Omphale and Hercules, Hercules being the god (Plutarch tells us) to whom Antony bore 'singular devotion to counterfeit and resemble him'. These happy memories are driven out by the news of Antony's marriage. The fishwife behaviour is more pronounced here, but Mr. Mason points out that the messenger has asked for trouble: more than the marriage, he has referred to the marriage bed. He had forgotten she was a queen, and she reminds us of this in her half-apology, 'Some innocents 'scape not the thunderbolt', and in her acknowledgment that she shouldn't have struck an inferior. This savagery is a part of Cleopatra, or of Cleopatra in love, and we admire as we deplore, some of us admiring more, others deploring more. The close of the scene is tersely moving, the more so, I find, in that Shakespeare doesn't offer to make Cleopatra more of a tragedy queen than she is, or less of a Cleopatra:

> *Bid you Alexas*
> *Bring me word how tall she is. Pity me, Charmian,*
> *But do not speak to me.*

Mr. Mason has some appreciative comments on the scene and its continuation (Act III Scene iii), and he says of the latter, 'It is only when . . . we note how her attendants humour her, that we feel for the first time that Cleopatra needs our sympathy.' The first time we could rightly feel that, I would say, is directly after her very first words in the play, following the harsh speech of Philo.

Cleopatra's description of Antony as one way like a Gorgon, the other like a Mars, though it is neither original nor particularly apt, at least should give us plain warning. If we want to hear about the divine love of two divinities, then we shall have to go elsewhere. If we maintain that the story of two imperfect people in imperfect love cannot by its nature engage our interests at all deeply and should be left to those many contemporary story-tellers who exploit such material, then we must simply cross *Antony and Cleopatra* off our list of plays to be visited.

The first part of the scene fulfils its purpose well enough—we had better see something of these great ones together—but the second part, between two of the lesser, is much livelier. Little needs to be said about it, but it contains pleasures which (to go no further) we cannot count on finding in many plays by other authors of the period. If we are to allow Enobarbus's death of a broken heart to affect our picture of Antony—and how should we not?—then we must expect him to be built up into a considerable presence. This glimpse of Enobarbus chatting as an equal with another soldier, but showing himself so distinctly the superior in wit, intelligence and address, contributes to that building up.

A little earlier the great men were planning to give one another feasts, and Pompey remarked snidely,

> *first or last,*
> *Your fine Egyptian cookery shall have*
> *The fame. I have heard that Julius Caesar*
> *Grew fat with feasting there.*

I want to break off here and consider L. C. Knights's interpretation of the play. He writes, 'The continued references to feasting—and it is not only Caesar and his dry Romans who emphasise the Alexandrian consumption of food and drink—are not simply a means of intensifying the imagery of tasting and savouring that is a constant accompaniment of the love theme; they serve to bring out the element of repetition and monotony in a passion which, centring on itself, is self-consuming, leading ultimately to what Antony himself, in a most pregnant phrase, names as "the heart of loss".'* On the charge of monotony we must hear the evidence of the protagonists, and that evidence weighs more heavily than the feasts and wine: Cleopatra is precisely *not* monotonous! As for the banqueting: the rich are not like us, they eat and drink more, or they used to. Because we are virtuous, shall there be no more cakes and ale? If you own a palace, you might as well use it, and banqueting appears to have been a custom in Egypt before Antony's arrival: Julius Caesar grew fat there.

But Professor Knights's argument that looking back we recall how often, apart from feasts and wine, 'this love has seemed to thrive on emotional stimulants', raises a more interesting and meaningful question. Though again it is one which beckons us further than we may want to go. These stimulants—not food or drink—what are they exactly? Lovers' talk, lovers' quarrels, dressing up in drag, wandering incognito and incognita through the streets at night, fishing, provoking jealousy by allowing a stranger to kiss your hand? I think we shall be hard put to it to decide whether these are stimulants administered to love or stimulations arising out of love and part and parcel of it. The distinction assumed here needs a close and arduous examination, and such an examination, I suspect, would produce some surprising (though inevitably tentative) conclusions. Take these things away, and what are the manifestations of love? What should a passion centre on but itself, for as long as it *is* a passion? I suppose it could be said that making love is an emotional stimulant on which love often seems to thrive!

SCENE VII

The galley scene is Shakespeare's comic writing at its best. Antony appears as a wit (his impersonation of an old

* *Some Shakespearean Themes.*

92

colonial hand is splendid), though since his foil is Lepidus, this is not saying very much.

Menas's proposal to cut the throats of the three world-sharers reflects belittlingly on all of them. On Antony—the great lover can so easily be disposed of; and on Caesar—the power politician can be so easily disposed of. But it reflects more damagingly on Caesar, because it makes the world he is out to win look a small thing and because the one who would cut their throats, as if in a drunken brawl, is a fellow seeker after power, not a rival lover. This is a gloss on Cleopatra's later comment, "tis paltry to be Caesar'. Moreover Caesar is saved rather humiliatingly by a grudging sense of honour in Pompey which we cannot be sure he would himself obey in similar circumstances. We would have more confidence in Antony.

ACT III SCENE II

More guying by Enobarbus and Agrippa at the beginning of the scene (ridicule of Lepidus) and again at the close (the case of Antony's rheum, a reappearance of the crocodile and its tears: 'What willingly he did confound, he wail'd'), with some high-level meaninglessness in between.

SCENE VI

Rome: and an unpretty picture of it. Antony is in disgrace for giving away chunks of the Roman Empire to his sons (little is made in the play of Cleopatra as the mother of Antony's children, but nothing at all is said of his children by Octavia: that marriage hardly seems to have been consummated), and Lepidus is deposed and imprisoned for having grown 'too cruel'. It only remains for the abandoned Octavia to make an appearance. When she does, that it is Caesar's pride which is offended rather than his fraternal love is made all too plain.

> *The trees by the way*
> *Should have borne men, and expectation fainted,*
> *Longing for what it had not. Nay, the dust*
> *Should have ascended to the roof of heaven,*
> *Rais'd by your populous troops . . .*

—the reminiscence here of Enobarbus's account of the populace gathering to see Cleopatra in her barge and the air which almost went too is cruel. The most interesting thing about this scene is what is not in it: Shakespeare doesn't stir up our sympathy for Octavia, and thus our feelings against Cleopatra. He allows her the barest commiseration—a little less of it and he would seem even hostile to her—and this he minimises by putting it chiefly in Caesar's mouth. The bald lines spoken by Antony in Dryden's play describe Shakespeare's effect in this connection:

> *Pity pleads for Octavia;*
> *But does it not plead more for Cleopatra?*

And of course there is much more than pity to plead for Cleopatra.

SCENE VII

> *A charge we bear i' the war,*
> *And as the president of my kingdom will*
> *Appear there for a man. Speak not against it,*
> *I will not stay behind.*

Here is Cleopatra being 'masculine'. She estimates incorrectly—as does Lady Macbeth—and her femininity

gets the upper hand. Enobarbus's objection to her presence, coarsely expressed *sotto voce* and then delivered in
decent translation, is sensible of course. Antony, alas,
striving to outdo Cleopatra in manliness, proposes to fight
by sea. Enobarbus is admirably firm and dignified: there
is no place for pleasantries in a serious matter like this.
Alongside Caesar's cold and single-minded prudence,
Antony's casualness (no wonder Caesar used to beat him
at sports!) has its attractive side, but the effect on morale
of his yielding to Cleopatra is plain enough. 'We are
women's men': the most hurtful thing Roman soldiers
could say of themselves. The effect of the remarks passed
by the 'worthy soldier' concerning the Egyptians and the
Phoenicians is to clinch the final feeling—that great-
heartedness shouldn't involve risking the lives of one's
followers. The outcome is unambiguous:

> *I never saw an action of such shame;*
> *Experience, manhood, honour, ne'er before*
> *Did violate so itself.*

Even so, I cannot agree to the implications—or perhaps I have grasped them wrongly—of what Mr. Mason
says at this stage. 'We might therefore well feel that had
Shakespeare been writing a free tragedy he would have
ended his play about here. And if he had treated Antony
as a supremely heroic figure there would be little more to
say. As it is, Shakespeare has drawn for us the degradation of the extinguished hero beyond the point where life
could ever be fully lived again.' Mr. Mason's last sentence, or something like it, could be said of Macbeth when
he has murdered Duncan: that *he* is certainly not going to
live life fully after this point is the tragedy of it! Is there
something in the basic situation, in the plot material,
which prevents us from feeling for Antony in the way
we feel for Macbeth? Is loss of honour in a military
man somehow more disgusting or antagonising, more

conclusive, than a noble's murder of his king? Is regicide more universally engrossing than a fatal love, and ambition inevitably nobler than passion? Did we *want* Antony to stay with Octavia? Or do we insist on an undegraded Antony, enjoying both Cleopatra and battle honours, finally killed in an honourable and soldierly action? Well, yes, some of us do. But, as Mr. Mason grants, 'some of the finest things in the play are just about to occur', and others among us are not going to let this 'degradation' prevent us from accepting them. We may even feel that without the degradation these things would not be.

SCENE XI

> *Let that be left*
> *Which leaves itself: to the sea-side straightway;*
> *I will possess you of that ship and treasure.*
> *Leave me, I pray, a little: pray you now,*
> *Nay, do so: for indeed I have lost command . . .*

Antony in defeat is quite a spell-binder. His generosity (though no doubt aided by guilt), his offer to his followers of a ship laden with gold, will presumably be understood as reasonably 'real', not as a flight of poetic fancy or a try-on of Shakespeare's, since it accords with his later behaviour towards Enobarbus.

The passage which develops with Cleopatra's entrance I find quite exquisite, though exquisitely painful. If it is not very noble, it is very human in Antony to evoke Philippi, to recall how once he was a better soldier than Caesar. The tragedy of shame, of this kind, is nearer to us, one would have thought, than Macbeth's tragedy of knowing his soul irretrievably lost by one single action which brings him absolutely nothing in return.

But now we come to a difficulty of interpretation. 'O,

whither hast thou led me, Egypt?' I had always found this passage deeply moving:

> *Egypt, thou knew'st too well,*
> *My heart was to thy rudder tied by the strings,*
> *And thou shouldst tow me after. O'er my spirit*
> *Thy full supremacy thou knew'st, and that*
> *Thy beck might from the bidding of the gods*
> *Command me.*

I saw, there, Antony not so much seeking to shift the blame for this particular disaster on to Cleopatra as acknowledging her power over him (and her knowledge of that power). (Again, is it worse to be overcome by love than by ambition?) It even seemed to me that for once Antony was rising above Cleopatra, for where he shows the dignity that can accompany self-knowledge even at such moments, she tells a silly little self-excusing lie: 'I little thought You would have follow'd.'

But Mr. Mason reads black where I read grey. Remarking that Antony falls from a lower height than does Macbeth, he adds that in one sense he falls to a lower depth: 'Macbeth never reproached his wife with instigating him to crime.' (But Macbeth *knew*, though the fact is not evident to us at first, that he was stronger than his wife.) Mr. Mason maintains that we can feel nothing but contempt for Antony when we hear him saying, 'Egypt, thou knew'st too well . . .' In support of his reading he could adduce the reiterated

> *You did know*
> *How much you were my conqueror . . .*

which is superfluous, meaningless except as an attempt to shift the blame. In support of my reading there is the swiftness of reconciliation, after so few words from Cleopatra:

> *give me a kiss,*
> *Even this repays me.*

What caused the loss repairs the loss. I think, though, it would be unfitting to push very hard the plea that, in blaming Cleopatra, at least Antony is taking her seriously: unlike Enobarbus in Scene xiii, and unlike the later Macbeth, whose attitude towards his wife takes on a rather patronising tinge. There is no good reason why Antony should take the Egyptian queen seriously as a soldier: the seriousness is of another sort.

It is not that Mr. Mason is wrong in his description of the state of affairs, but rather that his expectations are inappropriate, and relate to a play which would be so *different* from this one that the question of it being a 'better' play simply would not arise. Perhaps the right reading lies between our two extremes—this, we have noted, is a play which drives its commentators to extreme positions. Love in action is always changing its shape, ebbs and flows, is never to be assessed and held to the one shape once and for all. A military defeat, on the other hand, is something immutable and precise, it immediately becomes a piece of history. It would take a greater man than Antony not to blame love and therefore his lover for this permanent stain—and if Antony were a greater man then we would not have this play. If Macbeth were a greater man . . . If Lear were a greater man . . . If we were all greater men, there would be no tragedy at all.

Bradley (no Cleopatra-hater!) claims that Cleopatra 'ruins a great man, but shows no sense of the tragedy of his ruin'. It takes two, in these cases, to ruin either one of the two. And it would be asking too much of any woman that she should recognise her responsibility for a *tragedy* of this kind. Cleopatra has given Antony too much for that, and (to her way of thinking) the only real tragedy for which she could be held responsible would arise out of her ceasing to love him. Ruin of any other sort, in any other way, can appear only minor in comparison. And

Bradley himself finally acknowledges that all this seems to us 'perfectly natural, nay, in a sense perfectly right'.

SCENE XII

Caesar's 'policy' is to persuade or bully Cleopatra into driving her 'all-disgraced friend' out of Egypt or killing him there. She appears all the more remarkable when we consider the view of women which prevails hereabouts:

> *women are not*
> *In their best fortunes strong: but want will perjure*
> *The ne'er-touch'd vestal.*

The world seems to be full of her ill-wishers, and we could desire for her a protector stronger than Antony—but no, she is not really amenable to protection. Plutarch too shows her a remarkable person: even a blue-stocking, who could speak all sorts of languages, unlike her royal ancestors, who 'could scarce learn the Egyptian tongue only'. Shakespeare spares us this aspect of her: or spares Antony.

SCENE XIII

Enobarbus is implying much the same thing here: the *débâcle* was Antony's fault alone, he assures Cleopatra. It would be lowering to male pride to *allow* a woman any real share of the responsibility. 'What though you fled . . .'

Antony's challenge to Caesar to 'lay his gay comparisons aside' (a man who could use such language isn't extinguished yet!) and meet him sword to sword is foolish in that Caesar obviously won't accept it. And Enobarbus is sensible in seeing its foolishness. Whether we would be right to make merry over Antony's silliness is quite

99

another matter, however. Caesar, we may recall, declared at Philippi that he 'was not born to die on Brutus' sword', and Brutus then put down the 'young man' quite firmly.

Having been told that she had a right to be frightened in the battle, Cleopatra now displays fear in confronting Caesar's messenger. Caesar, she confesses docilely,

> *is a god, and knows*
> *What is most right.*

The sight of this natural fearfulness determines Enobarbus (though he thinks it natural for women to be afraid) to desert Antony:

> *Sir, sir, thou art so leaky*
> *That we must leave thee to thy sinking, for*
> *Thy dearest quit thee.*

We should observe that Cleopatra does not say she will drive Antony out of Egypt, let alone kill him; also, of course, that Thidias does not propose that she should. Thidias's way of putting it, unlike Caesar's in briefing Antony's ambassador in the preceding scene, is extremely tactful, fit for women's ears. He supposes it is fit to kiss women's hands.

Antony's fury is not pleasant to witness, nor his bombast to hear. The whipping of Thidias is an act of impotence, not of nobility however hard pressed. What excuse can be offered for him he proposes himself, when he says that Caesar makes him angry, 'harping on what I am Not what he knew I was', at a time when it is most easy to make him angry. As for the outburst against Cleopatra, here we have to enquire of ourselves whether, if we were given an account of love which had no jealousy in it, we would *believe* it. This is not *Romeo and Juliet* (a tale of good, healthy, appropriately young love, which students sometimes throw in the face of this play). And I don't think one has to be middle-aged to feel that *Romeo and Juliet*, though it has furnished us with convenient archetypes for young star-crossed lovers, is less than a great play. Antony and Cleopatra are not star-crossed, they are self-crossed and crossed by each other—they have had the *time* for that, unlike the lovers who die before their honeymoon is over; they are protagonists of tragedy, however precariously, whereas Romeo and Juliet are merely participants in what is loosely and popularly called 'a tragedy'—what a tragedy, so young, so handsome, so promising . . .!

Again, Antony's rage against Cleopatra does not last long; for it is not really rage against *her*. Despite the strained conceit and the awkward wording, I have always found her speech, 'Ah, dear, if I be so . . .', strangely resonant, charged with a mysterious power; it is something more than the expected assurance, the oath or promise, which it sets out to be: the speaker stands aside from the noise of revilement and expostulation, moving for a moment into another dimension.

> *so*
> *Dissolve my life; the next Caesarion smite*
> *Till by degrees the memory of my womb,*
> *Together with my brave Egyptians all,*
> *By the discandying of this pelleted storm,*
> *Lie, graveless, till the flies and gnats of Nile*
> *Have buried them for prey!*

This is a description of what will not happen, and it brings to mind her later references to 'the quick comedians' presenting 'our Alexandrian revels', something which *will* happen. There is the weight of centuries of history here, of the centuries which have passed since her, and the passage lends her an extra largeness as being part of recorded history. She and her womb *are* remembered; and we are made to remember that this human is a historical figure and conversely that history is made of human lives. We can only say, with Antony, 'I am satisfied'.

If we feel that the passage does have something of this effect, then we shall find Antony's rhetoric ('I will be treble-sinew'd . . .') rather less bombastic and silly.

> *I, and my sword, will earn our chronicle:*
> *There's hope in't yet.*

There isn't really any hope in it, in the sense Antony means: but he is right in the other respect: he has earned his chronicle. And in this play, which some find so deeply flawed and unsatisfactory, Shakespeare has given the chronicle a further lease of life.

Of course, Enobarbus is perfectly correct according to his own sublunary lights: 'Now he'll outstare the lightning . . .' But to deny that Enobarbus is the sole or final judge is not necessarily to commit oneself to the glorious apotheosis of Antony (or of Cleopatra, or of Antony-and-Cleopatra) which the more romantic admirers of the play have reckoned to find there. And, to stay fairly close down to earth, when Enobarbus states, in an accurate diagnosis,

> *A diminution in our captain's brain*
> *Restores his heart,*

I think we may fairly ask, what else is there for Antony? Isn't it something that his heart is—that it still can be—restored? As for Enobarbus himself, the reverse is going to prove the case: an increase in his brain, in his 'reason' (*v. iii. x.* 36), is going to lose him his heart.

ACT IV SCENE I

'The old ruffian': Caesar's description of Antony doesn't induce us to like Caesar any the more; 'there is a horrid aptness in the phrase,' says Bradley, 'but it disgusts

us.' Caesar is particularly hoity-toity in this scene.
Maecenas comes off better (and by implication rebukes
readers who expect Antony to behave with the dignity
bred by Sandhurst) when he comments,

> *When one so great begins to rage, he's hunted*
> *Even to falling.*

Caesar's

> *. . . tomorrow the last of many battles*
> *We mean to fight*

looks forward to the day after tomorrow, when Antony
is to lay the poor last of many thousand kisses upon
Cleopatra's lips.

SCENE II

Enobarbus is uncertain how to interpret Antony's farewell to his servitors. Is it 'one of those odd tricks which
sorrow shoots Out of the mind', or does he merely mean
'to make his followers weep'? Despite this last cynical
judgment, he too appears to succumb: 'I, an ass, am
onion-ey'd; for shame, Transform us not to women': and
Antony at once switches to a heartier tone. Even if we
sense something conscious and knowing about Antony's
charm, and find something obtrusively self-dramatising
and too distinctly self-pitying in his behaviour, he still
gains from the contrast with Caesar in the preceding scene,
who (reasonably but cold-bloodedly) proposes to place the
defectors from Antony in the van. It will be granted, I
think, that the tragic hero must be more than ordinarily
conscious of himself if he is to be fully conscious of his
own tragedy, of what is happening to him. Without this
consciousness there won't be any tragedy. Macbeth of

course is superbly (though less than accurately) aware of himself from the start, while Lear has to unlearn his awareness of himself as a king and learn awareness of himself as a man. And it is the element of the dumb ox in Coriolanus, I would say, which renders him so dubiously a tragic figure: at times he is being led to the slaughter, at other times he is making his own way there, but without much awareness of the direction he is taking. In *Antony and Cleopatra* as elsewhere in Shakespeare's greatest plays, and notably in *Lear* and *Hamlet*, we can occasionally see how the poet is hard pressed to convey a sufficiently clear and powerful sense of this searing awareness without also producing a distasteful side-effect of self-pity in his hero. Though I am loth to appeal to historicism, it remains a possibility that in ages less democratic, less levelling, than ours, this distaste would be less easily provoked; we are reluctant to acknowledge greatness in the first case, let alone to grant that on occasion the great may be greatly weak.

SCENE IV

A domestic scene, illustrating the 'correct' relationship between the two, as (with some perfectly proper fumbling at the outset) Cleopatra helps to arm her knight and her knight treats her as the little woman who quite properly doesn't truly understand the 'royal occupation' of war. Cleopatra sustains her role admirably well—the episode is further testimony to her 'infinite variety'—until she has received her 'soldier's kiss' and seen the men on their way. Then she comments, sadly and wisely,

> *He goes forth gallantly: that he and Caesar might*
> *Determine this great war in single fight!*
> *Then Antony—; but now—Well, on.*

If Antony were altogether dead in our esteem by now, surely his reaction to Enobarbus's defection would re-suscitate him!——

> *Say, that I wish he never find more cause*
> *To change a master. O, my fortunes have*
> *Corrupted honest men.*

Enobarbus has acted 'realistically': as a soldier he is simply saving his own life by leaving a doomed master, a master whose life he can now do nothing to save. As Edmund told the captain in *King Lear*, 'to be tender-minded Does not become a sword'. But then he realises, in the first place, that in fact his action is *not* 'realistic', for those who have defected to Caesar are treated harshly or at best without 'honourable trust'. Secondly, when his treasure arrives from Antony, he realises that his action is in a deeper sense unrealistic, because it goes against something in his nature: he cannot continue to lead the life he has so rationally saved.

> *I am alone the villain of the earth,*
> *And feel I am so most*

——he does not seek to blame anyone else, unlike Antony, yet his words dovetail with those spoken by Antony, when the latter reflects on how his fortunes have corrupted honest men, thus casting a warm glow of feeling on both men. Enobarbus does a lot for Antony by his death, and he does a lot for himself too; all in all he certainly 'earns a place i' the story'.

Mr. Mason, though, feels that something fishy is going on here. 'The theatregoer's question is whether anything in the play justifies Enobarbus' scruples and self-reproach. Can we point to behaviour in Antony that sets up the moral situation which Enobarbus both describes and implies? Does it come over us as we attempt to make up the necessary sum that Shakespeare is now beginning to attempt by mere telling to undo what he has shewn; that he is illegitimately restoring to Antony the heroic virtues he properly robbed him of?'

But if we are going to ignore Enobarbus's dying speech in Scene ix ('O Antony, Nobler than my revolt is infamous . . .'), then what are we not going to ignore? We *can* point to behaviour in Antony that is sufficient to set up the moral situation in question: and that we ourselves might not consider it necessary to die in these circumstances may merely indicate that we are less than Enobarbus was. Nor is it exactly a question of Antony's 'heroic virtues': it is rather his human virtues, co-existing as they do alongside human vices, which have brought the by no means hysterical Enobarbus to this. Were Antony characterised by heroic virtues solely, Enobarbus would never have left him and the question of heartbreak never have arisen. Once again, the complaint derives, I think, from a curiously grudging desire that art should be simpler and more straightforward, more a matter of black and white, than life is itself.

One comment on Mr. Mason's attitude would be that he has himself taken a notable part in this 'robbing' of Antony—and of Cleopatra, and of their play. He has thrown pieces of poetry out of the play, complaining on each occasion that there is nothing in the play to validate them dramatically. And on each successive occasion it has been easier to do this, of course, until finally there is little drama in the play because so little poetry has been left to it. The process is somewhat akin to a balloonist complaining that he is soaring helplessly into the vast inane while simultaneously casting out his ballast.

I can only suggest that it is possible for a man to be weak on one occasion and brave on another, to be petty-minded and yet also magnanimous. There seems to me nothing inherently unlikely, let alone disgusting, in the mixture of nobility and ignobleness, of heroism and foolishness, of dignity and feeble self-excuse, which is manifested in this dramatic character. If imperfect beings are not admitted to the region of the tragic, then tragedy must be something remoter from our lives than we have taken it to be.

SCENE VIII

> *What, girl, though grey*
> *Do something mingle with our younger brown,*
>   *yet ha' we*
> *A brain that nourishes our nerves, and can*
> *Get goal for goal of youth . . .*

Et cetera. Antony's bombastic speeches here are not surprising in one who suspected he was done for and now imagines for a moment that he is not. They are pathetic more than distasteful. Hysterical, yes, somewhat, but tragedy is not meant to be played *sotto voce*, and at least we see that Antony isn't altogether the dessicated wreck some critics would have him at this stage. He asks Cleopatra to give Scarus her hand to kiss, consciously or otherwise balancing the Thidias incident.

SCENES XII AND XIII

'All is lost . . .' More rant from Antony: 'the witch shall die'. The women are frightened, and their fright together with their wiles (they are certainly living up to the male view of women now!) lead them to the fatal plan of pretending that Cleopatra is dead.

SCENE XIV

Antony has recovered himself, and this scene is quiet and moving, except for the brief outburst evoked by Mardian's entrance.

> *I made these wars for Egypt, and the queen,*
> *Whose heart I thought I had, for she had mine . . .*

—again he complains, but he acknowledges his love even at a time when most men would be careful to deny or depreciate it. He believes that Cleopatra has 'false-play'd' him, and tells Eros,

> *Nay, weep not . . . there is left us*
> *Ourselves to end ourselves.*

It is impossible to tell how close he is to killing himself at this point, or, as regards the motivation for suicide, what proportion would arise from defeat as a lover and what from defeat as a soldier, the end of love and the end of power. But Mardian's report of Cleopatra's 'death' clinches the matter: it adds urgency, and of course a kind of joy (the joy of resolution, of single-mindedness) to his decision.

Eros's inability to kill Antony, his killing of himself instead, is further testimony to one kind of greatness in Antony (who would do this for Caesar?), working in the same way as Enobarbus's death. Undeniably Antony has one characteristic of the tragic hero: he does not leave this world unattended.

No rant from Antony when he hears of the deception, not a single angry word. In addition to his understanding of Cleopatra's fears, and of his own imminent death (he hasn't made that much of a mess of the job!), he displays

only a gallant stoicism—and much less of an inclination
to make his followers weep:

> *Nay, good my fellows, do not please sharp fate*
> *To grace it with your sorrows: bid that welcome*
> *Which comes to punish us, and we punish it*
> *Seeming to bear it lightly.*

ACT IV SCENE XV, ACT V SCENE I

'Here's sport indeed! How heavy weighs my lord!'
We remember 'O happy horse that bears the weight
of Antony!'

There are no words of reproach from Antony, but only
words of advice—together with a little self-praise,

> *the greatest prince o' the world,*
> *The noblest . . .,*

or rather praise of what he once was, which is perhaps for-
givable in a dying man. The beginning of this last speech
strikes the true tragic note, indeed it would be difficult to
find a better exemplar:

> *The miserable change now at my end*
> *Lament nor sorrow at . . .*

Of Cleopatra's lament,

> *O, wither'd is the garland of the war,*
> *The soldier's pole is fall'n: young boys and girls*
> *Are level now with men: the odds is gone,*
> *And there is nothing left remarkable*
> *Beneath the visiting moon,*

Mr. Mason comments, as we might expect, 'I am unable
either to feel it as generated out of her own mind or to relate it to the Antony of the play. The lines are written in
by Shakespeare, and it is a pity that he did not organise a
play around them.'

Together with this speech and the neighbouring passages—'the crown o' the earth doth melt', 'that huge spirit'—we may group the celebrated speeches in Act v Scene ii, opening with 'I dreamt there was an Emperor Antony'. We do not take all this *au grand sérieux*, nor should we assume that Shakespeare intends us to or hopes that we will. This is not the truth, the whole truth and nothing but the truth. It is Cleopatra's truth, or part of it, the part that matters most at this time. What would we think of her if she treated us to a cool measured appraisal of Antony, warts and all, at this juncture? Certainly (as those students would say, and as they say of practically every metaphorical expression) Cleopatra 'goes too far'. But then, there are times when it is only right and proper to go too far.

What puzzles Mr. Mason more ('and makes me wonder what Shakespeare thought he was doing') is 'the deliberate insertion of a favourable Roman epitaph for Antony' in Act v Scene i. 'We cannot mistake the author's intention here', says Mr. Mason; 'Shakespeare lets himself go in his self-indulgent delight in hyperbole and gives incongruously to Caesar the following words':

> *The breaking of so great a thing should make*
> *A greater crack. The round world*
> *Should have shook lions into civil streets,*
> *And citizens to their dens. The death of Antony*
> *Is not a single doom, in the name lay*
> *A moiety of the world.*

Before we tax Shakespeare with indulging himself we should look very carefully at what he is saying and think carefully about it, and it will not hurt if in this process we make use of what knowledge we have of human nature and behaviour. In this case, since Shakespeare is accused of indulging himself in hyperbole, a besetting sin of poets though now to be regarded as an old-fashioned one, we

should make sure that the words in question *are* irretrievably incongruous. We cannot expect Mr. Mason, who is
of the opinion that Antony died effectively during the first
scene of the play, to believe that 'the death of Antony Is
not a single doom'. But there are other considerations. The
speech is much the sort of tribute which Shakespeare's
more important dead are accustomed to receive. Coriolanus is given one, though somewhat hurried and grudging (but what, by then, was there left for anyone to say
about him?); Hamlet is granted a brief testimonial to his
promise; Brutus gets some notably kind words from
Antony; though Macbeth for the plainest of reasons
doesn't. And it would look odd if Caesar said nothing at
all: the theatre, by its nature, invites observance of the
social decencies. Moreover, this is the obituary which the
victor traditionally owes to the vanquished; and possibly
here, however little reflective he is in general, Caesar
thinks of the wheel of fortune and of the lion roaming in
the Capitol before his uncle's death. Agrippa remarks,

> *strange it is,*
> *That nature must compel us to lament*
> *Our most persisted deeds*

—meaning that, though it is 'strange', it is human and
common. And we would expect this particular obituary
to be more strongly worded or 'hyperbolical' than usual,
since it is the surviving triumvir who speaks, and in laud-
ing Antony, Caesar is glorifying himself as the conqueror
of such a great and belauded man, as the other moiety of
the world in whose name now lies the whole:

> *we could not stall together,*
> *In the whole world.*

In brief, there is nothing that obliges us—nothing is
trying to oblige us—to take everything we are told as being
literally true; nor are we required to suppose that Caesar
is speaking with total sincerity: it was not so long ago that,

in a reductive version of the words of Agrippa quoted above, Enobarbus remarked of Antony weeping for Brutus, 'What willingly he did confound, he wail'd.'*

Finally, both Maecenas,

> *his taints and honours*
> *Wag'd equal with him,*

and Agrippa,

> *you gods will give us*
> *Some faults to make us men,*

combine to modify the 'hyperbole' quite sharply.

SCENE II

What might more justly be objected to in this play is that it gives us too much, two tragedies instead of one, an embarrassment of riches. By and large literary critics are a conservative lot.

Cleopatra by herself. 'Quick, quick, good hands': there can be doubt as to the genuineness of her attempt to kill herself here. Proculeius unfolds a curious argument:

> *Do not abuse my master's bounty, by*
> *The undoing of yourself: let the world see*
> *His nobleness well acted, which your death*
> *Will never let come forth.*

---

* An earlier instance of this 'strange' but not uncommon element in human nature is Antony's reaction to the news of Fulvia's death in Act I Scene ii:

> What our contempts doth often hurl from us,
> We wish it ours again. The present pleasure,
> By revolution lowering, does become
> The opposite of itself: she's good, being gone,
> The hand could pluck her back that shov'd her on.

This, like his tears for Brutus, could be advanced as testimony of Antony's emotional instability; it could also be taken as indications of a natural and persistent (though not always dominant) generosity.

Cleopatra is to lend herself to the greater public glory of Caesar, in one way or another. For the word 'bounty' we merely substitute the word 'triumph'; and indeed Proculeius almost gives the game away when he speaks of letting the world see Caesar's nobleness 'well acted'.

The passage with Dolabella is, I find, most moving at the point where Cleopatra asks,

> *Think you there was, or might be such a man*
> *As this I dreamt of?*

Shouldn't this spike the critic's guns? She has remarked, on Dolabella's entrance,

> *You laugh when boys or women tell their dreams,*
> *Is't not your trick?*

She knows what to expect—what boys and women can expect—from men, from the men who remain in her world. Now her dreams stand in the level of their lives, of their realism, their 'reason'. Dolabella, at least, is moved by her grief.

We note that Caesar has a total disregard for grief: if Cleopatra kills herself, it will not be out of grief as far as he is concerned, it will be an attempt to make out that he, Caesar, is cruel. Caesar is ever the politician, for whom everything that anybody does is first of all a political act and to be judged as such.

The Seleucus episode often poses a problem for students and their elders alike. If Cleopatra really intends to die, why does she seek to deceive Caesar in the matter of her wealth? 'She would live on if she could', as Bradley puts it, 'and would cheat her victor too of the best part of her fortune.' John Dover Wilson argues, however, that she has planned this 'deception' with or without Seleucus so that Caesar will suppose she doesn't intend to kill herself, as a token of her continuing attachment to life and as gay a one as possible. Indeed, Caesar does 'approve' her 'wisdom in the deed' and, in his self-satisfaction, exhorts her not to blush for it: the deed is a sound political one, to his way of thinking, all the more acceptable in that it hasn't deceived *him*.

Dover Wilson adduces Plutarch, who tells us plainly that Caesar 'took his leave of her, supposing he had deceived her, but indeed he was deceived himself'. I believe that such was Shakespeare's intention, but Shakespeare has not made it plain. And if we are to import Plutarch into the play here, we may have to allow him in at other points, and the net result will certainly not be the greater glory of either Antony or Cleopatra. Yet I think Dover Wilson is right in suggesting a sense we get that Cleopatra is acting a part here. Her handling of the situation smacks of prior planning:

> *Say, good Caesar,*
> *That I some lady trifles have reserv'd,*
> *Immoment toys, things of such dignity*
> *As we greet modern friends withal, and say*
> *Some nobler token I have kept apart*
> *For Livia and Octavia, to induce*
> *Their mediation . . .*

This speech is so neat, it comes pat, it has the air of having been rehearsed: we find ourselves admiring the show she is putting up. However you interpret the scene, it is spirited: this is the old Cleopatra if not (in the background) the new one as well. Caesar is a clod by comparison. After his fine words—'Caesar's no merchant'—he tells her to 'feed, and sleep', as if she were a Strasbourg goose or a lamb fattening for the slaughter; he wants her in tip-top shape for his triumph. 'He words me, girls, he words me': she was always rather sceptical about fine words, at least until Antony died, and she is right here.

Certainly she doesn't want to be exhibited in Rome, but women are especially sensitive to public ridicule, and there is no call to feel that her concern for her dignity somehow

has the effect of belittling her love for Antony. It settles
the question, true—but why should we suppose that the
death of one lover necessitates the suicide of the other?
Shakespeare is giving us the 'full picture': and perhaps
that is what offends those of us who would rather have a
selective one. Can it be that Antony and Cleopatra are 'too
human', too much like us, to be true tragic figures? In that
case (if I may repeat myself) what or who is tragedy *for*?

> . . . *now from head to foot*
> *I am marble-constant: now the fleeting moon*
> *No planet is of mine.*

I see no reason for not believing her, especially since the
Clown now enters with a pretty worm concealed in his
basket as ordered. When she said, 'I have nothing Of
woman in me', she was using the language of men who
know what women are like, but when she says of 'the
curled Antony' that he'll make demand of Iras

> *and spend that kiss*
> *Which is my heaven to have,*

she is speaking the language of women who know what
men are like. A death-bed soaring into spirituality, a
transcendental exit, would be incongruous. Where Mr.
Mason says of the ending that Cleopatra 'has ceased to be
part and parcel of the real', I feel the opposite: that, resist-
ing (with ease) the temptation a lesser poet might have
yielded to, Shakespeare has sustained the reality he has
already created for us. Cleopatra will still be Cleopatra.
(And what a woman!—able to joke on the brink of death:
'Have I the aspic in my lips?' This approaches the idiom
of the stout Roman soldier.) It is also the language of
women, in an obvious way, when she says,

> *Peace, peace!*
> *Dost thou not see my baby at my breast,*
> *That sucks the nurse asleep?*

But even in death she is not safe from the determination of the critics to put her in her place. We are accustomed to the presence of evil in our tragedies: here there is nothing to satisfy our simple expectations, so we pick on Cleopatra as the next worst thing. Seizing upon Charmian's 'Your crown's awry'—for me, a nice touch to a lady-in-waiting's character; for him, almost a suggestion of a tipsy whore whose hat is about to fall off her head— Dr. A. P. Riemer talks of this 'reminder of her imperfection' which 'robs her royal death of a small portion of its magnificence and greatness'.* Like Antony, she couldn't even carry off her suicide with dignity! Dr. Riemer adds, in that coroner-like tone of voice we have heard elsewhere among the critics, that 'it is right and proper that Cleopatra should miss out on the finality of perfection she strives for'. To me this seems merely petty malice, another indication of how Cleopatra has managed to get under the scholars' skin.

L. C. Knights has to be taken more seriously when, acknowledging the power and beauty of the poetry hereabouts, he yet warns us against letting the poetry take its effect on us, against allowing it to 'obscure the continued presence of something self-deceiving and unreal. She may speak of the baby at her breast that sucks the nurse asleep; but it is not, after all, a baby—new life; it is simply death.' A metaphor is a metaphor, after all; a last brave joke is a last brave joke, and this one is finely in character. Cleopatra is not deceiving herself that the asp is really a baby, nor trying (why should she?) to deceive us into thinking that some 'new life' is beginning. There is no question of

* *A Reading of Shakespeare's 'Antony and Cleopatra'*, 1968. Adducing 'the vulgarity and passages of comedy' in it, Dr. Riemer tells us that 'this is, perhaps, the first iconoclastic play in English . . . Despite Shaw's belief to the contrary, this play is strikingly similar to *Caesar and Cleopatra.*' *Strikingly* similar? Strikingly *similar*? But as a whole Dr. Riemer's account of *Antony and Cleopatra* is more interesting, and less unfair, than those parts of it I quote would suggest.

life, new or old; it is not the babe who is sleeping but the nurse who is about to fall asleep, for ever; Cleopatra knows she must die (though what, by the by, is so 'simple' about death?); she dies in a most gallant manner. The more you consider it, the more astounding, the more splendid, this joke of hers comes to seem. Why should we go out of our way to spoil it? It is a bold man, or a strangely sanctimonious one, who is prepared to accuse someone about to die by her own hand of self-deception and unreality.

Cleopatra's ladies live up to her, or die up to her. Charmian speaks a brief epitaph, first for the 'lass unparallel'd', then for the 'princess Descended from so many royal kings'. Of this passage John Middleton Murry has written with a fervency I find allowable: ' "A *lass* unparallel'd." Who dare risk it? Who but the man to whom these things were no risk at all? Every other great poet the world has known, I dare swear, would have written, would have been compelled to write: "A queen unparallel'd" . . . There is the harmony between "Royal Egypt!"—and "the maid that milks". These two are blent in one in the phrase.'

But perhaps the best epitaph on Cleopatra is Caesar's, which follows the lead set by Cleopatra herself, and is more than a conventional tribute to a late empress, much more from the heart and more immediately apropos than his tribute to the dead Antony:

> *she looks like sleep,*
> *As she would catch another Antony*
> *In her strong toil of grace.*

His enemies once out of the way—his enemies, or those who lived a life irreconcilable with his, and had to be put down because his pride could not tolerate such anomalies —he speaks graciously; despite the loss to his triumph, he really seems to be *seeing* the woman he is looking at, and for the first time he shows himself as an attractive person.

*   *   *

Yet, 'we are saddened by the very fact that the cata-strophe saddens us so little; it pains us that we should feel so much triumph and pleasure', says Bradley, 'and the fact that we mourn so little saddens us.' But do we feel *so* much triumph, and do we feel an improper pleasure? I suppose in a sense we mourn more for Macbeth, for whom the world was ill lost and totally lost. But do we mourn (is that the right word?) much more for Lear? Perhaps we do, because we reckon that Cleopatra has had more out of life than he has had. Partly our grief for Lear derives from the spectacle of a lesson hard learnt and learnt too late to be of use (of use to Lear, that is), and there can be no question of Cleopatra having learnt a lesson: she has paid a price for what she has had. But then, perhaps we do mourn more for Romeo and Juliet (as Bradley claims) than for Antony and Cleopatra. And this prompts me to wonder whether this calculation of depths or degrees of mourning isn't rather mechanical and ex-cogitated, and beside the point. Bradley appears to admit as much in concluding that the play 'gives us what no other tragedy can give, and it leaves us, no less than any other, lost in astonishment at the powers which created it'. It would be a sad thing if we lost the ability to be lost in astonishment altogether; and to be so lost, in contempla-tion of the mature Shakespeare, ought not to signify any very disastrous loss of intellectual face.

At all events, I cannot say that it *pains* me to feel triumph and pleasure. And triumph, incidentally, is part of the state of feeling which *Lear* leaves us with. I would opine that *Antony and Cleopatra* is 'tragedy', is still 'tragedy', unless we are prepared to limit the definition of this term so severely that we have to invent another one for the sole use of this play.

'MACBETH'
and The Henpecked Hero

'MACBETH'
AND THE HENPECKED HERO

MACBETH is a single-minded play, uniquely so among Shakespeare's works, and there would seem to be little for the commentator to say about it at this time; very little indeed, compared with *Lear* and *Antony and Cleopatra*, two plays where the 'total situation' involves a more complicated arithmetic. Everybody admires *Macbeth*; nearly everybody has written about it.

And yet, to judge from the recurring confusions into which students fall, some problems still persist. The biggest of these—for if you go wrong here, you go wholly wrong—concerns Macbeth's responsibility or otherwise for the crime he commits, or the degree of responsibility to be attributed to him. Perhaps because their experience of literature runs ahead of their experience of life, students tend to conceive of evil as something large, vague and exciting, which exists outside of human beings, which is indeed too exciting, too momentous, to be at all closely attached to mere men and women, to be relevant to such creatures as their parents and teachers. For some of them the play should not be entitled *Macbeth*, but *Evil* or (in the case of the more pragmatic) *Disorder*.

For others it should be called *The Weird Sisters* or *Lady Macbeth*, since the former are not mere men or women and the latter (since first impressions count for a lot) is more a witch than a wife. Such readers will find G. Wilson Knight's commentary in *The Wheel of Fire* extremely congenial, since he begins with 'the inner state of disintegration, disharmony and fear, from which is born an act of crime and destruction', a state of mind to which he refuses to give so mean a name as 'ambition'. He stresses the notion of 'the objectivity of evil': evil 'comes from without', and thus it is, he maintains, that 'the Weird Sisters are objectively conceived'. Evil comes from without—as if it were some species of radioactivity emanating from another planet and unamenable to scientific investigation. The consequence of applying this conception of evil is that Macbeth can only be seen as the innocent victim of an epidemic or a traffic accident or, better, a collision with a meteorite. One would certainly not reproach Professor Wilson Knight with the cold-bloodedness found in some other twentieth-century critics, but here, in the good cause of bringing out the play's momentousness, he has simply reduced its significance. That we cannot praise 'the Gods', the supernatural powers, for dealing out unequivocal justice in the play of *Lear* is not sufficient reason for blaming them for the outbreak of unequivocal evil in the play of *Macbeth*. I am setting aside the shaky theory which has it that assent on the part of the spectator to the irresistible potency of the supernatural solicitings will have the advantage of allowing Macbeth to retain, or in some way, usefully seem to retain, a large slice of his 'original' nobility of character.

One of the teacher's concerns, then, will be to save Macbeth from shrinking under the influence of metaphysical magic into a poor little man (whose clothes do not fit!), henpecked by his wife, by the Weird Sisters, and by Evil Absolute and Disembodied. Another, however, will be to save him from that reading of the play which leads students to answer the good old question, 'Do you consider that Macbeth is an absolute monster?', with a simple though wordy 'Yes'. It is even possible that Macbeth will have to be defended against both views simultaneously, when he is seen as an absolutely monstrous, henpecked weakling.

*   *   *

Whenever a short sketch is needed for Prize Day, the Weird Sisters are exhibited; whenever the script of a film involves a scene of amateur dramatics, we are shown the Weird Sisters. They must be the most acted, the worst acted, and the most frequently guyed trio in the history of the drama. And when they are portrayed most seriously they will seem to be most outrageously sent up. We take the significance of the line 'Fair is foul, and foul is fair', the first statement of one of the main themes of the play, etc., but it seems to me that we pay a large price for that significance, a significance generally weakened, moreover, by the agents who convey it.

But we pay a heavier price if we argue this way: the witches may seem ludicrous to us, because we know better than to believe in witches, but the people for whom Shakespeare wrote believed in witches and took them very seriously, and perhaps he did too, and if we put ourselves in their place then . . . Then before long Macbeth appears as the helpless and rather boring little pawn of objective and absolute evil indicated above.

The Weird Sisters are 'objective', not only because Shakespeare's audience would enjoy seeing them (that much darkness we must allow to the dark ages!), but because it is dramatically more powerful that Banquo should also see them, so that we can compare his reactions with Macbeth's. In a similar way it is dramatically right that no one but Macbeth should see the Ghost of Banquo, and it is right that, once Macbeth is dead, the Weird Sisters are not seen again because there is no one left to see them. As with the manifestations of poltergeists, their 'objectivity' is quite severely limited.

Whatever the modern reader or playgoer may feel about them, they are in the play. The important fact to

note is that from the outset their powers are fairly clearly
restricted. For one thing, there is the childishly bogey-
man idiom in which they converse. It is only when
Macbeth is among them that they are at all impressive:
it is he who gives them stature, as he gives them significance. Left to themselves they are fairy-tale figures de-
signed to frighten young children but not too badly. 'I'll
do, I'll do, and I'll do.' But what do they do? A sailor's
wife has declined to hand over her chestnuts—it's a poor
sort of witch who can't conjure up her own chestnuts!—
and so the Weird Sisters decide to avenge themselves on
her by tormenting her husband. They have the winds at
their disposal, by tradition, it seems; but on their own
admission they do not have the power to destroy and kill:

> *Though his bark cannot be lost,*
> *Yet it shall be tempest-tost.*

If they cannot destroy an anonymous sailor, it is unlikely
that they would be able to destroy a great man like
Macbeth. If they are supposed to reinforce the play's
theme of unnaturalness and horror, then the theme must
be badly in need of reinforcement.

Coleridge goes to the heart of the matter when he insists
on the early birth-date of Macbeth's guilt. Remarking
rather quaintly that 'superstition, of one sort or another, is
natural to victorious generals', he points out that the object
of these scenes of superstition is not to excite but 'to mark
a mind already excited'. Though the witches cannot
drown a sailor, they can incite a man to do that which he
is already tempted to do. In itself, as Kenneth Muir puts
it, their prophecy of the crown is 'morally neutral'.*

> *Good Sir, why do you start, and seem to fear*
> *Things that do sound so fair?*

* Introduction, Arden edition, 1953.

What can Macbeth's start indicate, as Coleridge says, but 'guilty thoughts'? And the contrast with Banquo should make this clear to us: he neither begs nor fears their favours or their hate. 'Are ye fantastical. . .?' This is surely the obvious and innocent question to ask, whether in Elizabethan England or medieval Scotland or here and now, and Coleridge describes the situation well when he says that Banquo's questions are 'those of natural curiosity, —such as a girl would put after hearing a gipsy tell her school-fellow's fortune;—all perfectly general, or rather planless'. In contrast Macbeth's questions do not have an air of planlessness; he wants to know the authority of the Weird Sisters:

> *Say from whence*
> *You owe this strange intelligence?*

Macbeth has to argue with himself—it is of the play's essence that he must talk himself, with difficulty, into action—but he does not start with a blank page. If his mind were virgin, he would have heard and taken in what Banquo says about the mode of procedure of 'the instruments of Darkness'. These latter tell us truths the better to harm us, they

> *Win us with honest trifles, to betray's*
> *In deepest consequence.*

Immediately after this speech of Banquo's, Macbeth admits that the supernatural soliciting cannot be good because it brings the idea of murder into his mind, yet tells himself that it cannot be ill because it has contained a truth, to the effect that he would become Thane of Cawdor. It may be held that Macbeth didn't hear Banquo's advance demolition of the latter part of his argument because he was engrossed in his own thoughts, and thus Banquo is simply explaining the true position to the audience. But Banquo is here speaking directly to

Macbeth, in reply to a specific and weighty question ('Do you not hope your children shall be kings . . .?'), and my own interpretation is that Macbeth hears but prefers to reject Banquo's assessment because it is not convenient to him. After all, by granting that there is something not 'good' in the matter of the predictions, he contrives to allow himself to believe that he has paid his debt to truth and conscience. He goes on to pay his debt to common sense, too:

> *If Chance will have me King, why, Chance may*
> *   crown me,*
> *Without my stir.*

And his fourth and final aside also sounds sensible—

> *Come what come may,*
> *Time and the hour runs through the roughest day*

—if less unambiguously apropos. But it is to turn out less than true, later, when

> *To-morrow, and to-morrow, and to-morrow,*
> *Creeps in this petty pace from day to day,*
> *To the last syllable of recorded time . . .*

It is only grown-up children who can believe that the witches are 'embodiments of evil'. They are embodiments of something entirely human—man's gift for persuading himself or almost persuading himself that something he wants to do is the right thing to do. What they 'objectify' is our aptitude for self-deception in varying degrees. The real evil, the truly terrifying things, are to be met with not in the Weird Sisters or in the quaint revelations of Rosse and the Old Man, but in the speeches of Macbeth and Lady Macbeth. The play is certainly not the static object that its description as 'a statement of evil' would imply. 'Statement' is just a good, clean, up-to-date, business-like, unromantic-sounding sort of word, which means a good deal less than it seems to, for everything is a statement of something or other. *Macbeth* is an unparaphraseable exploration and experience of evil, a direct involvement in the evolution of evil, and of evil in the only place we meet it—in man. Evil is what Macbeth does to himself, we observe and experience it most keenly there, in Macbeth, and in a sense there is something to be said for the recurrent student who, in a mighty effort to be charitable, declares that 'after all, anyone might kill a king . . .'

Returning to Scene ii, 'A camp': I sympathise with those who have doubted its authenticity. Modern critics, I suspect, are keen on it because it fits in with the 'blood' imagery theme. 'What bloody man is that?' Kenneth Muir notes that it has been calculated that 'blood' is mentioned over a hundred times in the play. Much of the verse in this scene is of an extremely low standard (the line about memorising another Golgotha rears up like a mountain), and the bloodiness is rendered in the coarsest and most conventional way.

The picture of Macbeth which we are treated to is not a pretty one: 'Bellona's bridegroom', with his 'brandish'd steel, Which smok'd with bloody execution', unseaming the enemy 'from the nave to th' chops'. It is not solely because Duncan is old that we cannot imagine him described in such terms. Macbeth is a man of violence, and of course the robust heartiness of his violence here contrasts nicely with the reluctance and fearfulness of his violence against the King. But one should be on one's guard against one's own dislike of violence and killing. (Scholars, we may note in passing, are generally much less acutely worried by bloody slaughter than by Cleopatra's wantonness.) A good warrior is one who kills as many as possible of the enemy in as short a time as possible. At present Macbeth is serving Duncan, and this does seem a 'holier' war than any of the fighting encountered in *Coriolanus*, for example.

L. C. Knights says that this scene, located in Duncan's palace, the war over, 'suggests that natural order which is shortly to be violated' and 'stresses natural relationships . . . honourable bonds and the political order . . .'* Yes, but . . . For one thing, 'stressing the natural order' in any direct way is always a rather thankless undertaking. 'Order' is most acutely desired when disorder prevails, it is rarely appreciated otherwise; and I do not think Shakespeare was quite the happy voice of the establishment that some critics have supposed him to be. For another thing, the scene opens with talk about an execution, which is never a cheerful topic. 'Natural order' and 'natural relationships' have their price. And in fact a good deal of sympathy is worked up for Cawdor, though this could be read to fit in with Professor Knights's account of what is happening: the wicked Cawdor has become 'natural' again ('very frankly . . . confess'd his treasons, Implor'd your Highness' pardon . . .'), acknowledged the 'political order', and died a good death.

Duncan's disquisition on how there is no way of deducing a man's cast of mind from his external appearance is interrupted by the entrance of Macbeth. In retrospect this incident would seem to contribute to an atmosphere of confusion rather than to any adduction of natural order. Critics have remarked often enough on the irony arising out of Macbeth's appearance at this point in Duncan's moralising, and I mention it only because one can hardly not do so. It is part of what I have called Shakespeare's single-mindedness in this play that he should seize on every opportunity of making his point, or of directing our attention to it, whether through such simple devices

* 'How Many Children Had Lady Macbeth?', 1933, in *Explorations*, 1946.

as this (which elsewhere we might well consider arrant crudeness) or in the complex speeches of Macbeth. Single-mindedness is not of course inevitably the same as simple-mindedness.

> *O worthiest cousin!*
> *The sin of my ingratitude even now*
> *Was heavy on me. Thou art so far before,*
> *That swiftest wing of recompense is slow*
> *To overtake thee: would thou hadst less deserv'd . . .*

Duncan is unrestrained in his expression of gratitude.* But Macbeth, as Coleridge pointed out, speaks constrainedly, in 'the language of effort':

> *Your Highness' part*
> *Is to receive our duties: and our duties*
> *Are to your throne and state, children and servants;*
> *Which do but what they should, by doing everything*
> *Safe toward your love and honour.*

He sounds almost like Cordelia for a moment. The fact remains that we wouldn't admire him either if he were more effusive. Macbeth fails to prevent himself from deceiving himself; but he is not any ordinary sort of hypocrite, he lacks the low gifts required to deceive others.

> *Stars, hide your fires!*
> *Let not light see my black and deep desires;*
> *The eye wink at the hand; yet let that be,*
> *Which the eye fears, when it is done, to see.*

E. F. C. Ludowyk points out, as others have done, that the stars which Duncan has just invoked as shining on all

---

* A minority of readers, having avoided the traps described earlier in this chapter, and wishing to justify or extend the respect they rightfully feel for Macbeth, argue that Duncan's gratitude is all too unrestrained and that, having been so exalted and then led to anticipate even more, Macbeth can properly expect to become Duncan's successor, and is thus normally and rightfully aggrieved when he hears Duncan proclaim Malcolm as his heir. But it would be perverse to penalise the King for his royal generosity, and we cannot entertain for long the idea that Macbeth's claim to the throne has any normality or legitimacy about it.

deservers in the form of signs of nobleness are promptly bidden by Macbeth to extinguish themselves.* 'Order', I have suggested, is best defined, as well as most highly esteemed, when it is absent; and the same holds true of 'natural relationships'. These four lines of Macbeth's tell us more about order and relationship than does the rest of the scene. And his few resonantly poignant lines in Act v Scene iii,

> *And that which should accompany old age,*
> *As honour, love, obedience, troops of friends,*
> *I must not look to have,*

tell us more on the subject than the whole of this scene. Of 'this night's great business', John Holloway writes, 'What seemed like the beginning of everything was in fact the end of that, and beginning of nothing.'† 'Nothing', as Macbeth comes to know it, is necessarily expressed by him in terms of loss of 'everything', and here more forcibly than anywhere else is 'everything' defined.

SCENES V, VI AND VII

How very different from Macbeth's is the language of Lady Macbeth! It is highly euphemistic—on the way to euphuistic—and abstract and undefining. Thus, 'what thou art promis'd' (the kingship), 'the nearest way' (murder), 'pour my spirits in thine ear' (like an angel of inspiration), 'the valour of my tongue' (also like an inspiring angel, but meaning, 'encouraging to murder'), 'all that impedes thee' (in the first case the continued existence of Duncan), 'metaphysical aid' (the Weird Sisters, described earlier by Banquo as 'so wither'd and so wild in their attire', and later by Macbeth as 'secret, black, and mid-

---

* *Understanding Shakespeare*, 1962.
† *The Story of the Night*, 1961.

night hags'), and of course the strange inverted euphemism, made to sound derogatory in spite of itself, 'th' milk of human kindness'. A quite remarkable instance of circumlocution is

> *thou'dst have, great Glamis,*
> *That which cries, 'Thus thou must do,' if thou have it;*
> *And that which rather thou dost fear to do,*
> *Than wishest should be undone.*

All this, as Professor Ludowyk says, is 'a form of magic' (but self-deluding), 'as potent as that of the Weird Sisters'. More potent, I would say, though ultimately as impotent.

This is a kind of language which Macbeth cannot rise to. He is earthbound in comparison.

We also notice that, in her euphoria, Lady Macbeth talks of '*my* battlements'. The theme of 'unsex me here' and 'take my milk for gall' is resumed a little later, in Macbeth's presence, with 'the babe that milks me'. She is in fine fettle to bolster up her husband's resolution when he arrives; she is quite ready to direct the operation herself:

> *you shall put*
> *This night's great business into my dispatch . . .*

And the only thing Macbeth is given a chance to say is 'We will speak further.' The false assessment of the relative claims of the two to be the real hero/villain of the play is understandable in that Lady Macbeth gets off to a flying start.

In the following scene we perceive that she is far more fluent, not to say elegant, in her expressions of loyalty to Duncan than was Macbeth:

> *All our service,*
> *In every point twice done, and then done double,*
> *Were poor and single business, to contend*
> *Against those honours deep and broad, wherewith*
> *Your Majesty loads our house . . .*

A trifle reminiscent of one of Lear's other daughters, perhaps, but well turned: 'We rest your hermits.' Macbeth trudges some way behind her. He is still trudging, or wading, long after she has fallen to earth and smashed herself.

The contrast between these two is as pointed in the next scene as it could well be. 'If it were done, when 'tis done . . .' In his magnificent soliloquy, Macbeth pronounces all the correct answers to his own questions, as Banquo had answered correctly his question about the goodness or illness of the supernatural soliciting. And, again, he doesn't quite give those answers the complete credence which would finally dissuade him from the murder. They are, of course, none the weaker for that: only Macbeth could make with such potency the point that 'He's here in double trust . . .' The offence contemplated presents itself as ranker than Claudius's, even though the latter 'hath the primal eldest curse upon't'. Nothing that anyone else can say will add materially to Macbeth's own particularisation of the evil which lies ahead of him. This is emphatically *not* euphemistic language: 'assassination', 'this blow', 'bloody instructions', 'even-handed Justice', 'poison'd chalice', 'his kinsman and his subject', 'bear the knife myself', 'the deep damnation of his taking-off', 'the horrid deed', 'vaulting ambition'. Incidentally, it is difficult to understand G. Wilson Knight's insistence (though one sees its connection with his theory of objective or external evil) on Macbeth's 'ignorance of his own motive': that Macbeth is so pre-eminently a self-conscious being is central to the play, and moreover we know when he is lying or mistaken, and clearly he is neither at this point.

Compared with this soliloquy, Lady Macbeth's first speech was in a foreign language. If there is any delusion here, it is in the opening lines, when Macbeth gestures with an easy defiance in the direction of 'the life to come', for that objection is quickly 'jumped'. The awkward truth is that we still have judgment here, or so Macbeth will find, and not merely in this world here, but here in the King's palace, 'here, But here', indeed, with the ensuing and apt punishment of becoming a king who is no king. 'The effect of the language', as D. H. Rawlinson says, 'is to make us realise how little Macbeth is able to visualise a neatly worked-out, deftly executed and unpunished crime.'*

With the entrance of Lady Macbeth, the intellectual level of the discourse drops markedly. Macbeth at this moment has talked himself logically out of the murder; his wife now talks him illogically back into it. His reasoning has been slow and careful, painstaking and private; her 'reasoning' has a different sort of power, it is 'theatrical', emotive, demagogic, as if she were addressing a mob, not speaking to a man, let alone a husband. Like all effective orators, she is quite ready to play foul:

> *From this time*
> *Such I account thy love.*

She remains circumlocutory in her phrasing:

> *Would'st thou have that*
> *Which thou esteem'st the ornament of life . . .*

She invokes the harmless and homely adage of the poor cat; she persists in abstractions:

> *to be more than what you were, you would*
> *Be so much more the man,*†

and even her ferocious talk of dashing the baby's brains

---

* 'Early and Late Shakespearean Verse', *The Practice of Criticism*, 1968.

† How much cannier was Volumnia, in addressing her son!—

> You might have been enough the man you are,
> With striving less to be so . . .

out (a contingency which is never going to arise) ends in another polite circumlocution:

> . . . *had I so sworn*
> *As you have done to this.*

Nevertheless, such is the power of her outburst that many a student fails to give Macbeth's brief interjection its proper and weighty due:

> *I dare do all that may become a man;*
> *Who dares do more, is none.*

The protagonists here display two different conceptions of 'a man'. Macbeth is contending that a man can be bold and daring only up to a certain point, and thereafter he becomes not-a-man, a beast, and some other word than 'brave' will then have to be found to describe him. Lady Macbeth's theory is of an altogether more primitive kind: a man ought to be daring, and the bolder he is the more of a man he becomes, bolder and bolder, more and more of a man, *ad infinitum*. She has no inkling of those limits set upon humanity which Macbeth was pondering over before she entered. 'Macbeth is never in doubt of the difference between good and evil', says Kenneth Muir, 'nor is Lady Macbeth . . .' I should say she is at this stage oblivious to the distinction, and to this blindness she owes her vast initial potency. Despite her terrifying gestures, she is quite a simple creature, and we ought to be able to tell now that the greater and more lasting human interest is to be located elsewhere, in Macbeth. Lady Macbeth of course is more active at the moment, or promises to do more, because for her 'doing' is such an easy matter. 'Probably in no play of Shakespeare are so many questions asked', writes G. Wilson Knight. 'Amazement and mystery are in the play from the start.' But we have to make a notable exception in the case of Lady Macbeth, who is unaware of mystery and quite unamazed except by her husband's mysterious scruples.

This fortitude of hers is what Coleridge called 'mock'. His thumb-nail description of her is well worth quoting in full: 'a class individualised:—of high rank, left much alone, and feeding herself with day-dreams of ambition'— Coleridge was not afraid of that lowly word!—'she mistakes the courage of fantasy for the power of bearing the consequences of the realities of guilt'.

'Bring forth men-children only!' cries Macbeth admiringly, the imaginative admiring the unimaginative. He is going to need male heirs. But it takes a woman to bring forth children, even so, and oddly enough Lady Macbeth's ferocious and unfeminine outbursts in this scene do accentuate the fact simultaneously that she is and remains a woman. It is brought out that here is a potential mother of future kings of Scotland, well equipped in every way for that role—or in every way but one. A. C. Bradley says of this couple, 'They are born to rule, if not to reign';* and the tragedy of Macbeth is, of course, that he is exactly fitted by nature for the throne, but he can only attain the throne by means which exactly unfit him for it.

'*Macbeth* is a terrible play,' says Arthur Sewell, 'because its business is to give us some notion of what that damnation is which a man embraces when he is, indeed, man enough for it.'† It is worth reminding oneself how difficult a thing this is to do, and how superbly it is done here, this portrait of a man eminently qualified to be a king, and eminently disqualified too. It is distressing in the extreme that the effect of recent criticism, by stressing the theme of little-man-dressed-in-borrowed-and-over-size-robes, has been to encourage students to suppose that all they see is disqualification, presumptuousness, ludicrous imposture—the sort of common situation which would not require Shakespeare's special powers for its creation and exploration.

* *Shakespearean Tragedy.*
† *Character and Society in Shakespeare.*

ACT II SCENE I

The hallucinatory dagger is sometimes interpreted as an extra seduction on the part of the Weird Sisters, thus further diminishing Macbeth's responsibility for what he is to do. But 'Thou marshall'st me the way that I was going' can well mean more than Kenneth Muir's annotation: 'The dagger seems to move towards the room where Duncan sleeps.' It can mean: 'You are encouraging me in the act which I was going to commit in any case.' This fits in better with the following line—'And such an instrument I was to use'—since the instrument is linked more intimately with the act than with the victim's whereabouts. Moreover, the idea of a moving dagger, like a carrot in front of a donkey's nose, would detract sadly from the dark dignity of this scene. The 'air-drawn dagger' of Lady Macbeth's scolding speech in Act III Scene iv can be 'drawn on the air' as well as 'drawn through the air', or perhaps better, since it comes directly after a reference to 'the very painting of your fear'.

SCENES II AND III

> *That which hath made them drunk hath made me bold:*
> *What hath quench'd them hath given me fire.*

But drink, as we are about to hear, is an equivocator, it gives one the lie. What Lady Macbeth has achieved is that equivocal condition of 'being so much more the man' which she recommended to her husband recently.

At the same time,

> *Had he not resembled*
> *My father as he slept, I had done't*

—this is an indication of some resistance in herself,

Bradley remarks, as he asks us to try to imagine Goneril speaking these words.

Having killed Duncan, Macbeth asks a question:

> *Will all great Neptune's ocean wash this blood*
> *Clean from my hand?*

and answers it,

> *No, this my hand will rather*
> *The multitudinous seas incarnadine,*
> *Making the green one red.*

What happens is similar to the incident in Act i Scene iii, where Banquo answers Macbeth's question as to whether the supernatural soliciting can be ill in advance of his asking the question. Here Macbeth is the juster reasoner. A moment later Lady Macbeth enters with her pathetic assertion, already rejected by him: 'A little water clears us of this deed.' The interrelation of the play's parts is even tighter, for Bradley notes that she doesn't suspect that her facile realism will one day be answered by herself: 'Will these hands ne'er be clean?'

Macbeth's acknowledgment of the personal disaster to himself which accompanies the murder of Duncan is prompt enough to come:

> *To know my deed, 'twere best not know myself.*
> *Wake Duncan with thy knocking: I would thou*
> *couldst!*

It was there all along. The situation between the evil which impelled him towards the crime and the intimate recognition of that evil which would dissuade him from the crime is *almost* comparable to the meeting of irresistible force and immovable object. Robert Bridges was not alone in believing that the Macbeth who felt the horror of the deed as clearly as Shakespeare's hero would not be able to commit it. One can sympathise with this point of view: Bridges was *nearly* right. The terror of the play lies in the fact that, when all is thought and felt, Macbeth is still just able to commit the deed. No offence against psychological truth is involved; for one thing, the actual commission of the deed is quickly carried out, and the very ease of the physical operation commends it to one who is involved in an arduous nightmare of horrible imaginings and agonising calculations. If we pause to admit the complexity of any human psychology worthy the name, perhaps we shall find that Shakespeare was simply being 'realistic' once again.

But when it is done, it is not done. And in the following scene, after the discovery of Duncan murdered, Macbeth must find a certain relief in speaking words which are both publicly and privately appropriate:

> *Had I but died an hour before this chance,*
> *I had liv'd a blessed time . . .*

For in its private aspect this is only a recurrence to the truth of Act I Scene vii:

> *He hath honour'd me of late; and I have bought*
> *Golden opinions from all sorts of people,*
> *Which would be worn now in their newest gloss,*
> *Not cast aside so soon.*

The irony here is more than 'dramatic', there is no invitation for us to feel superior over Macbeth's 'unconscious condemnation' of himself. What we might with slightly more reason feel superior about is Lady Macbeth's determined casualness after the murder—

> *These deeds must not be thought*
> *After these ways: so, it will make us mad*

—but if we do, we owe much of our superiority to Macbeth and his relentless awareness of 'this even-handed Justice' and of the truth that there is no anodyne against thinking, except perhaps sleep—and he has murdered sleep.

SCENE IV

The earlier part of this scene, with its superstitious Old Man, is certainly very folk-loristic and colourful. But, unnatural as is the deed that's done, the *play* does not tell us that Macbeth is a mousing owl who has hawked at and killed the falcon Duncan. We have not seen Duncan as a falcon, exactly, nor have we seen Macbeth as a mouse-chasing owl. We have seen something of Duncan as a good, indeed an irreproachable, and rightfully installed king. It would be nearer the mark to envisage Macbeth as one of Duncan's horses, beauteous and swift, the minions of their race, who has 'turn'd wild in nature . . . contending 'gainst obedience'. Except that Macbeth is following his nature here, part of it, in seeking to turn his potentialities into actualities. My feeling is that this passage between Rosse and the Old Man is an instance of Shakespeare wanting to make our flesh creep—though it could be considered a moot point as to whether he was writing for his present groundlings or for his future commentators. ''Gainst nature still . . .'

ACT III SCENE I

Thou hast it now, King, Cawdor, Glamis, all,
As the Weird Women promis'd; and, I fear,
Thou play'dst most foully for't; yet it was said,
It should not stand in thy posterity;
But that myself should be the root and father
Of many kings . . .

Bradley is of the opinion that Banquo 'has yielded to evil', and G. Wilson Knight says that, 'enmeshed' (truly enough) 'in Macbeth's horror', he 'keeps the guilty secret, and lays to his heart a guilty hope'. The position is uncertain, but I do not see any plain yielding to evil here. Banquo has his suspicions and, the only lord to know of the prophecies, he has said nothing and done nothing. But in this atmosphere of confusion and suspicion, who would believe him, or believe him usefully? Perhaps he cannot be more severely blamed for his prudence than Macduff is to be blamed for his costly imprudence. Macduff's family is destroyed, but not Macduff himself; Banquo is murdered, and his son escapes by an accident. Certainly Banquo bears a very favourable and weighty testimonial from Macbeth:

> *in his royalty of nature*
> *Reigns that which would be fear'd: 'tis much he dares;*
> *And, to that dauntless temper of his mind,*
> *He hath a wisdom that doth guide his valour*
> *To act in safety.*

And though one might wonder about the wisdom described in such terms, there is little evidence for, and no point in, making a case out against him.

We note Macbeth's plain cognisance that he has 'fil'd my mind' and 'mine eternal jewel Given to the common Enemy of man': it is now simply a question of how much he is getting in return.

L. C. Knights believes that Macbeth's catalogue of dogs, in his address to the two Murderers, 'stands as a symbol of the order that Macbeth wishes to restore'. This, I think, is a little over-ingenious, yet there may be a hint of a sort of nostalgia: any usurper, having disrupted order, will want to restore it, with the difference that he is now to be at the top. But more obviously, and primarily, Macbeth is meaning to stir up the Murderers by implying that they are special men to whom he is entrusting a special responsibility. Even hired thugs have pretensions which their employer will do well to respect. Gervinus pointed out that in appealing to 'manliness', Macbeth is employing the technique which his wife used upon him. Even though the passage may strike us as a small *tour de force* bearing slight relation to the play, one would not wish it away. It provides a nice little picture of Macbeth putting on the dog—showing who is king, or at any rate, who can speak like a king, even if only in front of paid assassins.

Another instance, perhaps the most moving, of Macbeth's splendid alertness to himself and the basic and continuing justness of his judgment:

> *Better be with the dead,*
> *Whom we, to gain our peace, have sent to peace,*
> *Than on the torture of the mind to lie*
> *In restless ecstasy. Duncan is in his grave;*
> *After life's fitful fever he sleeps well;*
> *Treason has done his worst: nor steel, nor poison,*
> *Malice domestic, foreign levy, nothing*
> *Can touch him further!*

The speech of which this is part begins in a mood of despondency ('We have scorch'd the snake, not kill'd it'), moves into one of strained resoluteness ('But let the frame of things disjoint': he would have the universe fall apart before he should suffer from—what in fact he *is* suffering from—fear and nightmares), and ends with this marvellously poignant evocation of the peace which only death can bring. A little later, typically, he finds 'There's comfort yet', the comfort largely deriving from the equivocal theory that 'things bad begun make strong themselves by ill'.

The snake has again been scorch'd, not killed. Or, as Macbeth puts it this time, the grown serpent is dead but the worm has escaped. Macbeth's reaction is,

> *Then comes my fit again: I had else been perfect;*
> *Whole as the marble, founded as the rock,*
> *As broad and general as the casing air:*
> *But now, I am cabin'd, cribb'd, confin'd, bound in*
> *To saucy doubts and fears.*

It is another fine illustration of the desperate will to delude oneself by telling oneself that one little thing will ensure complete and unequivocal and final success—or that, but for the one little thing that has gone awry, the whole big thing would have been a total and final success. It is true, here, that Fleance's escape leaves the undesirable prophecy open to fulfilment, and so is not exactly a small matter. But even if Fleance had been killed along with his father, Macbeth would be worrying over the possibility of Banquo's having sired a bastard unbeknown to him. There will always be something to bring Macbeth his fit again, to ensure that he doesn't gain his peace.

Lady Macbeth's mild reproach, after the Murderer has left, is unintentionally apposite:

> *My royal Lord,*
> *You do not give the cheer: the feast is sold,*
> *That is not often vouch'd, while 'tis a-making,*
> *'Tis given with welcome: to feed were best at home;*
> *From thence, the sauce to meat is ceremony;*
> *Meeting were bare without it.*

Macbeth and his wife could have lived pleasantly 'at home', in Inverness, as the Thane of Cawdor and his lady. There is no point in their 'dining out', in their being king and queen, if 'ceremony' is to be missing. 'Honour, love, obedience, troops of friends . . .', as Macbeth sees it, or, as the Lord in Act III Scene vi sees it, 'to our tables meat, sleep to our nights . . . Do faithful homage, and receive free honours.' And Macbeth has murdered ceremony—as the apparition of Banquo's Ghost illustrates in the very plainest way.

> . . . *the time has been,*
> *That, when the brains were out, the man would die,*
> *And there an end; but now, they rise again,*
> *With twenty mortal murthers on their crowns,*
> *And push us from our stools. This is more strange*
> *That such a murther is.*

This is a good touch. No one is more likely to resent un-natural happenings than the man who has been directly responsible for one, no one is more prone to complain of being pushed from his stool at the dinner table than the man who has seized a throne, no one is more indignant at the appearance of a ghost than the man who made it.

'Are you a man?' asks Lady Macbeth, and then, 'What! quite unmann'd in folly?' She does not see the Ghost her-self, she merely recalls the earlier success of this tech-nique. And eventually he replies to her, 'What man dare, I dare', and we are back in Act I Scene vii. 'I dare do all that may become a man . . .': Macbeth has offended against that excellent guiding principle, and it is too late now for him to invoke it in his own defence. Having yielded to his wife's theory of the inexhaustibility of daringness, he will now have to dare *more* than what man dare, and it is vain for him to cry out for mere Russian bears, armed rhinoceroses, Hyrcanian tigers and other such natural species.

It is evidence of his courage and (though total hardness is never reached) of his hardening that having reflected that 'blood will have blood'—and it is another fine human touch that the occasional speaking of plain truth should bring relief even to a man in his position—he quickly pulls himself together, 'What is the night?', and moves on to thoughts of Macduff. And of course we remark, as a sign of his continuing though sterile intelligence, the negative nature of the reason he gives for the further killings he anticipates:

> *I am in blood*
> *Stepp'd in so far, that, should I wade no more,*
> *Returning were as tedious as go o'er.*

ACT IV SCENE I

'Liver of blaspheming Jew', 'nose of Turk, and Tartar's lips', 'scale of dragon, tooth of wolf', and 'a tiger's chaudron': a recipe from the with-it witches' cookbook. The Weird Sisters have progressed in a dreary sort of sophistication since we last met them, and their hell-broth is horrific enough—but what is it *for*? I suggested earlier that it was only the presence of Macbeth among them which gave them stature. On this occasion they detract from his stature somewhat, by eliciting from him a bad piece of rhetoric:

> *Though you untie the winds, and let them fight*
> *Against the Churches; though the yesty waves*
> *Confound and swallow navigation up;*
> *Though bladed corn be lodg'd, and trees blown*
> *   down . . .*

And so on, through rather too many 'thoughs'. We take the point that his reference to Nature's germens tumbling all together is a true expression of his state of mind, that state more finely indicated a little earlier in the speech,[6] I am in blood . . .'

The Third Apparition's assurance,

> *take no care*
> *Who chafes, who frets, or where conspirers are,*

is a nicely deceitful adjunct to Macbeth's own reflections on the peace he has procured for Duncan:

> *nor steel, nor poison,*
> *Malice domestic, foreign levy, nothing*
> *Can touch him further!*

And Macbeth's response to these 'sweet bodements'—that he will

> *live the lease of Nature, pay his breath*
> *To time, and mortal custom*

—is going to be drastically modified by him in Act v Scene iii:

> *I have liv'd long enough: my way of life*
> *Is fall'n into the sere, the yellow leaf . . .*

The comfort he lays to himself after witnessing the show of kings is typical of him, and consonant with a man of considerable greatness of nature who cannot recognise the defeat he sees in front of him:

> *From this moment,*
> *The very firstlings of my heart shall be*
> *The firstlings of my hand*

—as if the trouble is simply that in the past he hasn't acted *promptly* enough.

SCENE II

One student, though able to find considerable extenuation for Macbeth's other actions, drew the line here: 'When he kills Lady Macduff and her son, he has gone down hill completely, and he forfeits all my sympathy.'

So perhaps this scene is required for the sake of those who might otherwise see nothing in the play to distinguish it from the stories of *coups d'état* which they read regularly in their newspapers. Perhaps L. C. Knights is making the same point when he maintains that 'There is much more in the death of young Macduff than "pathos"; the violation of the natural order is completed by the murder.' The pathos is ill prepared for by the child's cuteness and precocity; and, if anything, it seems rather less unnatural to kill him than to kill good old Duncan. As for 'nature', the only reference to it in this scene is made by Lady Macduff and concerns Macduff:

> *Wisdom! to leave his wife, to leave his babes,*
> *His mansion, and his titles, in a place*
> *From whence himself does fly? He loves us not:*
> *He wants the natural touch . . .*

SCENE III

Professor Knights proposes that the long passage between Macduff and Malcolm serves to 'emphasize the mistrust that has spread from the central evil of the play', and also, more importantly, performs the function of 'choric commentary'.* That it emphasizes mistrust is true (and if mistrust and worse hadn't spread from the central

* In the first version of *How Many Children Had Lady Macbeth?*, Professor Knights wrote, 'Falstaff is not a man, but a choric commentary.' In that this is true—that is, Falstaff is a character in a play and he does comment directly and indirectly on the actions of the play—it is clearly invidious to raise any objection. However, after contending with so many students who repeat the 'choric commentary' tag without having formed more than the haziest idea of what Falstaff is *like*, one feels obliged to move some sort of objection. Perhaps the best way of doing so is to claim that Falstaff *is* a man, and one well worth the slight trouble of getting to know. He cannot be any kind of effective choric commentary without being a man in the first instance: because we, who observe him, are men. When we know what sort of man he is—and, to be on the safe side, one had better make clear that this doesn't require us to examine him as rather an Historic

evil, then this latter would be either not especially central or not particularly evil), though whether mistrust needs to be emphasized at such length is another matter. As for 'choric commentary', it is surely not the case that what is at issue is so complicated as to require elaboration in this form, for the play is already its own sufficient commentary. Lust, incidentally, is not one of Macbeth's vices, as far as we know, and we must suppose that Malcolm's granting to him of this sin as of every other sin 'that has a name' enables Shakespeare to show the nature of royalty, as Kenneth Muir puts it, by describing its opposite in every respect. Again, in this play the exercise seems super-erogatory. And, somewhat comically, Macduff doesn't seem to think that lust in a monarch is a very grave dis-qualification anyway: 'We have willing dames enough'. For a fraction of a second we wonder a little about that natural order which prevailed under Duncan.

For me this whole passage is the one notable exception to the play's rule of immediate relevance, sustained economy and speed of evolution. It is the sort of 'filler' one would expect from a lesser dramatist, one who could never have written the rest of *Macbeth* and so wrote this instead. One has to add the rider, though, that quite a lot of the verse could only have been written by Shakespeare: for example, the speech beginning 'A good and virtuous nature may recoil, In an imperial charge . . .' Even so, one wishes the passage were over sooner, for one wants to

---

than a Dramatic being—when we know this, we shall understand what sort of a commentary he is delivering. This is the order of events, and there is no short cut.

Another favourite formula makes much of Falstaff's derivation or partial derivation from the Vice of the old plays. The interest of Shakespeare's plays arises less from the fact that they inherit something from the moralities than from the fact that they are so different from the moralities. You hardly praise Shakespeare by talking of morality elements in his work: but it would be great praise indeed to describe a morality play as having some-thing Shakespearean about it.

have done with choric commentaries and get back to Macbeth.

For that reason one would like Rosse to come out more quickly with his news; though this feeling does not prevent us from resenting Malcolm's insensitive attempts to pull Macduff together: 'Dispute it like a man.' And yet, we remind ourselves, if it were not for that shocking remark, we would be lacking the lines,

> *But I must also feel it as a man:*
> *I cannot but remember such things were,*
> *That were most precious to me.*

Bradley believes that Macduff's 'He has no children' refers to Malcolm, and we may well feel that in return for his inordinately business-like suggestion that they should all go and find comfort in revenge, Malcolm does deserve some such plain reproach. Even so, it is much more likely that Macduff is thinking of Macbeth, with the meaning that since Macbeth is childless, no adequate revenge is possible: a savage but natural thought. (The third alternative—that if Macbeth had had children of his own he could never have killed Macduff's—is clearly out.) At this stage, and despite the provocation offered, Macduff is not going to direct his bitterness against Malcolm, his new sovereign. Manners argue against that interpretation; common sense suggests he would have Macbeth foremost in his mind when he speaks the words; and we, in whose thoughts Macbeth is still foremost, who wish to return to him, are more than ready to see Macbeth, the childless usurper, brought before us.

ACT V SCENES I, II and III

Lady Macbeth's apparent superiority over Macbeth in 'strength'—in resolution, courage, fortitude—was the sign of an inferiority in imaginative subtlety and insight into human nature. That it was no real strength is obvious now. Lady Macbeth was a sprinter in evil; her husband, slower to get off the mark, is the long-distance runner—and he continues to run though he knows that the prize is irrecoverably lost. What (though he tried to smother his knowledge) Macbeth knew to begin with, that 'who dares do more, is none', Lady Macbeth has to learn, and the lesson kills her. She is walking in her sleep, talking of Banquo and the smell of blood, at a time when Macbeth has 'almost forgot the taste of fears'. It touches us that in this scene she should be seeking still, in between her direct cognisances of horror ('the Thane of Fife had a wife . . .'), to comfort and sustain her dream husband.

Menteth's words about Macbeth in the following scene are worth more attention than they generally get:

> *Who then shall blame*
> *His pester'd senses to recoil and start,*
> *When all that is within him does condemn*
> *Itself, for being there?*

They modify, I think, the oft-quoted lines of Angus which they follow, about the giant's robe hanging loosely upon a dwarfish thief.* What is good in Macbeth would not be 'there', in the company of evil, in Dunsinane, but at home, in the man who was briefly Thane of Cawdor, in Inverness. Essentially Macbeth is self-condemned, condemned by that which is within him, just as his actions were self-performed, not thrust upon him by wife or witches. As

---

* In his *Approach to Shakespeare,* D. A. Traversi remarks, 'Before the advancing powers of healing good, evil has shrunk to insignificance.' It hasn't. If it had, then it would not be evil: and Macbeth would be a bore. The natural tendency of critics to espouse the cause of good often ends in the relegation of evil to a trivial but handy little device for the demonstration of goodness, in the way that beggars enable us to demonstrate the beauties of charity—as if, in this case, the play would better be called *Duncan,* or perhaps *Malcolm.*

Professor Knights says, in pouring the sweet milk of concord into hell, Macbeth is at the same time 'violating his own nature and thwarting his own deepest needs'. But he will not crack up. He is more of a hero, in the lay sense of the word, than Antony; but his heroism is sterile and dry: it enables him, or it compels him, to live—to live to realise in utter fullness how he has managed to kill himself.

'The devil damn thee black, thou cream-fac'd loon!' In the midst of his bustling, the truth comes out again: 'I have liv'd long enough . . .' He says all this with so much more force than do his enemies, than Angus, for instance: 'Those he commands move only in command, Nothing in love.' His insight into the consequences of his actions is so much more intimate, felt and actual, than the insight shown by the victims of those actions. The evil he has committed never begins to shrink into insignificance; nor does he.

Of Macbeth's speech, 'If it were done, when 'tis done', D. H. Rawlinson says that 'Whatever he tells himself, he still *feels* morally.' This holds true, I would say, throughout the play. But, as John Holloway has pointed out, there is not really much question of Macbeth's *repenting*. Apart from the ambiguousness of their intent, his words to Macduff,

> *But get thee back, my soul is too much charg'd*
> *With blood of thine already,*

cannot carry that sort of weight. Repentance will not wake Duncan or the others, in any case, nor will it save Macbeth's soul in any sense of saving which we can conceive: it is one of those things like honour, love, obedience and troops of friends, which he cannot look to have. 'He does not affect more piety than he has', said Thomas Whately in 1785. And we are not in need of overt professions of remorse to prevent us from considering him a callous monster. It is difficult to imagine any expression of repent-

ance which would not lessen the fearful admiration we
have for this lost man.

> *She should have died hereafter:*
> *There would have been a time for such a word . . .*

Such is its context that her death, now, can signify nothing. There can certainly be no troops of mourning friends
in attendance. But the appropriate 'hereafter', the time
in which her passing could have meaning, will never come,
never would have come. Like Macbeth, she should have
died heretofore, 'an hour before this chance'—as the rest
of the speech admits fairly plainly. Granted that the sense
of the first two lines is obscure, yet we can be sure that this
is no simple callousness on Macbeth's part. Sometimes,
wishing to show their sensitiveness to the heinous nature
of his crime, students insist that among other things it has
(no doubt through its 'violation of the natural order') led
to the breakdown of the holy matrimonial relationship
between Macbeth and his wife. For not only has Macbeth
in a most unhusband-like manner kept things from her
('Be innocent of the knowledge, dearest chuck, Till thou
applaud the deed'), but he even finds himself too busy to
attend decently to the news of her demise. To this curious
and grudging complaint, Bradley offers the best short corrective: '. . . if as time goes on, they drift a little apart,
they are not vulgar souls, to be alienated and recriminate
when they experience the fruitlessness of their ambition'.

'Yet I will try the last . . .' Macbeth goes out to die with
harness on his back. The good are victorious, and we

accept that they should be. Order emerges from disorder, truth from deceit, as the critics point out zealously, and as no doubt they should. John Holloway says that at the close there is 'much emphasis on a movement of regeneration, a restoration of good at the level of the body politic'. But he is using the close of *Macbeth* to make manifest by comparison the sombreness, the austerity, even taciturnity, of the close of *Lear*. *There* we simply would not be able to endure talk of regeneration and restoration. At the end of *Macbeth* we can—we can endure it, indeed we accept it as the proper thing, the right note to end on. All the same, I do not think that, uninfluenced by the order-mongers, we are really very interested, vitally engaged, in this victory of Malcolm and the forces of good. Chiefly, it is a means whereby Macbeth can die, as die he must. It is his end that we care about, not a happy ending or a new beginning. The time is free, life goes on, and Scotland shall have its first earls—but the play is over. We withhold assent to the description, 'this dead butcher, and his fiend-like Queen', and altogether we are content to see very little of King Malcolm compass'd with his kingdom's pearl, and nothing of him being crowned at Scone.

'THE WINTER'S TALE'

More Tragedy than Comedy,
more Realism than Romance

'THE WINTER'S TALE'
MORE TRAGEDY THAN COMEDY,
MORE REALISM THAN ROMANCE

I N the opening scene the two gentlemen tell us two
things; the first (which Archidamus professes to find
too difficult to tell) is that the Bohemians have been treated
munificently during their long stay in Sicilia, and the
second is that the two kings are old and loving friends.

> Sicilia cannot show himself over-kind to Bohemia. They were
> trained together in their childhoods, and there rooted betwixt
> them then such an affection which cannot choose but branch
> now.

Derek Traversi finds an ominous equivocation here, since
while the word 'branch' signifies 'the unity of living
growth', it can also imply 'a spreading division within that
growth'.* But this is surely an instance of commentator's
tic, for there is no doubt as to what Camillo means and no
reason to suppose that Shakespeare means anything other
than what Camillo means: the good word 'root' does not
lend itself readily to a bad interpretation of its associated
word and derivative, 'branch'. A small matter—yet there
are always students who, fascinated by some alleged am-
biguity, will spend an essay on it to the neglect of the
rather larger remainder of the play. Archidamus's response, 'I think there is not in the world either malice or
matter to alter it', is of course going to look grossly ironic
in retrospect. But this is a stock device for heralding in a

* *Shakespeare: The Last Phase*, 1954.

155

sudden reversal of a situation apparently firm and immutable, and its economy may excuse its obviousness.

We are also informed of the existence and promise of Mamillius; and an irony of a finer kind evinces itself in Archidamus's comment (rather clumsy in itself, since he is repeating Camillo's words with little variation or added point) that if the king had no son, his subjects would desire to live on crutches till he had one. It is the king himself who is going to live on crutches till he recovers his daughter.

SCENE II

> *Nine changes of the watery star hath been*
> *The shepherd's note since we have left our throne*
> *Without a burden . . .*

It must be 'possible' for Polixenes to be the father of Hermione's child. At the same time Polixenes should not have stayed away from his own country for too long, especially since he is to profess fears 'of what may chance Or breed upon our absence'—and nine months already seems a long holiday for a king, since we are not to envisage Bohemia as a pastoral paradise requiring no governmental attention. Polixenes must stay in Sicilia for a minimum of nine months, also, if he is to have to escape just before the birth of the child and by his escape increase both Leontes' rage and his conviction of his justness to the point at which he casts out the baby. The timetable is inevitably an embarrassment; perhaps we could have wished that Polixenes had stayed for ten months or for eleven . . . While the continuous and high-minded symbolic interpretation of Mr. Traversi relieves the mind of such mundane worries, it also, I fear, relieves the mind from engaging in the play at all vitally, for while we can enter into Leontes and Hermione, we shall be hard put to it to get inside a symbol.

And why must Polixenes depart *now*—'that's to-morrow'? The country that can look after itself for nine months can do so for ten, and then Polixenes will be able to stay for the birth of the child of his two dear friends. The argument resolves itself thus: if a stay of ten months would make us feel a little easier about Leontes' jealousy by not requiring an immediate act of adultery, nevertheless Polixenes' proposal to depart before the birth can also be interpreted by Leontes as a sign of guilt and shame—and the more so in that it takes the mother-to-be to prevail upon him to stay longer.

To Leontes' pleas to delay his departure, Polixenes replies,

> *There is no tongue that moves, none, none i' th' world,*
> *So soon as yours, could win me: so it should now,*
> *Were there necessity in your request, although*
> *'Twere needful I denied it. My affairs*
> *Do even drag me homeward . . .*

That seems definite enough, and it would not be surprising should Leontes experience a little irritation at being told by his wife that 'You, sir, Charge him too coldly . . .' It ill befits one king to tell another that his country doesn't need him.

Like Lady Macbeth, Hermione is a more fluent talker in company than her husband; like Lady Macbeth, she uses her sex as a weapon. By 'a lady's Verily's As potent as a lord's', she means it is more potent. And faced with a choice of being her prisoner or her guest, Polixenes gives in.

As Coleridge says, the yielding of Polixenes is 'perfectly natural from mere courtesy of sex, and the exhaustion of the will by former efforts of denial'. It is also, as he says, 'well calculated to set in nascent action the jealousy of Leontes'.

This jealousy commences in a natural way and as a minor feeling of resentment. Hermione has persuaded his old friend to stay, where 'at my request he would not'. That is, Leontes is jealous not of Polixenes in relation to Hermione, but of Hermione in relation to Polixenes. But jealousy can start in one place and quickly spread to another: like cancer, it does little to announce itself, and it travels fast and far. In his excellent analysis of its development, Coleridge found the delineation of jealousy in Leontes more authentic and complete than in Othello.* Readers in general have found the account of its growth in the play impressive: it is, I would say, the greatest thing here, compelling almost to the point of nausea, and quite impervious to the most assiduous symbolists. Symbols attach themselves to the flower speeches of Perdita with much more ease, it seems, than to the agonised and agonising speeches of Leontes; they thrive where significance is lacking, not where meaning is unmistakably present. There will be nothing in the play to balance these dreadful speeches of Leontes until we arrive at the silences of the statue scene at its end.

What has drawn complaint is not the portrayal of jealousy in action, which is clearly masterly, but its suddenness, the absence of motivation, of 'cause'. For some readers this is the gravest of the play's famous improbabilities. I doubt whether these improbabilities strike us when we witness a performance of the play: I even doubt whether they strike us while we are reading the play. I fear they are part of that greater understanding of Shakespeare which we derive less from his works than from his critics, or which the necessity of setting or answering examination questions requires from us. As regards this present matter, we should ask ourselves what we would like Shakespeare to have done—as, in reading Mr. Mason,

* The passage, in 'Notes on *The Winter's Tale*', in the Everyman edition, *Essays and Lectures on Shakespeare*, is well worth studying.

we occasionally ask ourselves what he would have liked Cleopatra or Antony to have done or been instead of what they did do or were.

Would we like a handkerchief to be lost and found—a warning to all good wives that they look well to their linen? Do we want another Iago here, or another Iachimo? Would we like to have a Doctor, to explain to a Gentleman, in the well-intentioned way of J. I. M. Stewart, that more needs Leontes the Freudian than the physician, since he is projecting upon his wife the homosexual desires he must repudiate in himself?* Do we want—could we stand—a month or so of Hermione flirting innocently with her guest while Leontes trails them through the palace grounds, muttering obscenely to himself?

The contemplation of jealousy long-drawn-out is not only tedious but disgusting too, and however horrible Leontes' behaviour—and whatever truth may be in J. H. P. Pafford's estimate that 'he has none of the kingly graces listed by Malcolm'†—he must remain enough of a king and enough of a man to be capable of repentance, of performing that sixteen years of 'saint-like sorrow'. It would not do for us to sit and watch him laying traps for the supposed lovers, for instance. Moreover, while Hermione is rather tactless in her innocence, she must not be other than innocently tactless, there must be no sort of provocation offered by her. And something to the same effect must hold true of Polixenes too.

On the other hand, do we really feel inclined to view Leontes as G. Wilson Knight sees him (and substantially as he saw Macbeth), as the victim of absolute and objective evil, his jealousy unmotivated, himself 'a study of almost demonic possession'?‡

The real defence of Shakespeare's procedure is this:

* *Character and Motive in Shakespeare.*
† Introduction, Arden edition, 1963.
‡ 'Great Creating Nature', *The Crown of Life*, 1947.

jealousy can be largely or even totally 'irrational' in its
genesis, it can start from nothing, or from something at
all events incapable of detection in advance. We should
not expect necessarily to predict something which is in its
essence unpredictable. Once jealousy has come into existence it displays its own brand of 'logic', and with the help
of this insistent pseudo-rationality it accelerates in growth
at a rate beyond computation, for everything, commission
and omission alike, serves as grist to its mill. In complaining that Leontes' jealousy is 'merely frantic and—which is
worse in drama—a piece of impossible improbability',
Arthur Quiller-Couch was revealing a curiously innocent
view of human nature.*

Leontes' jealousy, Hermione's sixteen years of with-
drawal, the survival of Perdita and her discovery by
Florizel—these things are no more impossible, no more
unsusceptible to belief I would have thought, than the
atomic bomb or the Vietnam war, than mothers aged five
or murderers aged eleven. I am acquainted with the theory
that art has higher standards as regards credibility than
life, that fiction dare not admit itself to be as strange as
truth, and that all sorts of things which happen in reality
cannot be allowed to happen in the higher reality of art.
But I sometimes suspect that this theory is a conspiracy
promoted by academic critics in order to confine the
subject-matter of art within boundaries convenient to
themselves. What encourages me in this suspicion is the
fact that each of the plays discussed in this present book—
and they are by general consent among the author's best
—has been found 'improbable'. Lear's division of his
kingdom on the ludicrous principle of 'who says she loves
me the most gets the most' . . . Macbeth's acute sensitiveness to the peculiar horror of the murder he contemplates
most 'improbably' combined with the ability none the less
to commit that murder . . . As for Antony and Cleopatra,

* Introduction, New Cambridge edition, 1913.

it is not merely that they perform or incorporate improbabilities but that they are simply impossible—
phantasmal products of a dishonest legerdemain on the
part of 'poetry' . . .

More temperate than mine is Arthur Sewell's argument in writing of Leontes' jealousy: 'We can only understand Shakespeare's characters so long as we agree that
we can not know all about them and are not supposed to
know all about them.'* The imagination boggles at the
unthinkable thought of a play or novel which told us all—
and well it might, for there would be nothing left for the
imagination to do. And that in turn would mean there
would be no point of ingress for the reader, no opportunity for that necessary degree of identification. But in
this respect there would not seem to be a fundamental
difference between art and life, since for the majority of
us the number of real people whose characters we 'know
all about' must be very small indeed! Again, it might
appear that, while with one hand we extend to art various
concessions which we call 'conventions', with the other
hand we seek to elicit from it a greater 'realism', a greater
degree of 'knowing all about', a more consistent
'psychology', than we ever expect from reality or life
itself.

Yet it is better to worry about alleged improbabilities
and inconsistencies than, as some critics have done and
some students do, to maintain that they don't matter,
because this is only 'literature', or even that they are
positively admirable, the proper concomitants of a special
genre of drama. E. C. Pettet says of the plots of the
romances that 'with realism jettisoned, extravagance becomes a virtue'.† My own account of *The Winter's Tale*
would be the antithesis of this: where realism matters,
realism is not jettisoned; where there is extravagance, the

* *Character and Society in Shakespeare.*
† *Shakespeare and the Romance Tradition*, 1949.

play's grip on me is temporarily loosened. Mr. Pettet's view of these plays is analogous to the eccentric optimism of the man who, having fallen downstairs and broken his back, tells himself that he can now look forward to a nice ride in an ambulance: 'as the price that we pay for our far-fetched romantic stories we must accept behaviour and motives that are quite incredible and sometimes, as with Posthumus and Hermione, inconsistent with the disposition of the particular character concerned'.

In this matter of Leontes I would venture that Shakespeare is being *realistic*. True, Perdita's story is not a common happening, nor do unjustly accused wives often disappear from society for sixteen years.* But the jealousy portrayed in Leontes is by no means *outré* in its nature, nor is the remorse which succeeds, and nor are Hermione's thoughts and feelings at each stage of the action. If you feel that, in what truly matters, Shakespeare is being realistic, that the realism in *The Winter's Tale* far outweighs the much-discussed 'fairy-tale elements', then you will experience little compulsion to translate the play into abstract symbolism, to supplant the substance by the shadow. The basic defect (or of course advantage!) of symbols is that they are inevitably *crude* accounts of what they profess to describe or signify; their relation to the meaning of the work (assuming that the work is a successful one, for symbols are at their happiest in the vicinity of artistic failure) is more tenuous and enervated than the connection between the average student's paraphrase and the poem he is paraphrasing. Symbols, at the best, are shorthand, and Shakespeare wrote in long-hand. 'I rather

* The term 'fairy-tale', like the word 'myth', has acquired two distinct and indeed contrary meanings. In 'The Criticism of Shakespeare's Late Plays' (*Scrutiny*, 1942; *The Common Pursuit*, 1952), F. R. Leavis singles out the meaning which justifies the application of the term to elements in *The Winter's Tale* when he says, 'What looked like romantic fairy-tale characteristics turn out to be the conditions of a profundity and generality of theme.' I would stress the word *generality* here.

like symbols,' said a colleague of mine, 'they are so much easier to understand than people.'

How should Shakespeare account for Leontes' jealousy, for a diseased condition of the mind which psychologists have failed to explain in lengthy treatises, or have only explained at the price of raising yet other problems to be explained? Those readers are wiser who cite Camillo:

> *I am sure 'tis safer to*
> *Avoid what's grown than question how 'tis born.*

And we ought rather to admire the speed with which Shakespeare has portrayed the speed with which jealousy grows, the self-punishing pleasure the subject takes in distorted self-examination, his insistence on a scrupulous 'fairness' or false reasonableness and on not jumping to conclusions which he then feels free to jump to (like Macbeth scrutinising the goodness and illness of the initial prophecies), his self-pity, which excuses him from having to feel pity for anyone else, his delight in cryptically tendentious remarks which will enable him to save face without any risk of losing it—and also the real agony which is at the heart of this nightmare, for though perhaps the very greatest love is free from jealousy, we should not assume that genuine love will inevitably preclude it:

> *Too hot, too hot!*
> *To mingle friendship far, is mingling bloods.*
> *I have* tremor cordis *on me: my heart dances,*
> *But not for joy—not joy. This entertainment*
> *May a free face put on, derive a liberty*
> *From heartiness, from bounty, fertile bosom,*
> *And well become the agent: 't may, I grant:*
> *But to be paddling palms, and pinching fingers,*
> *As now they are, and making practis'd smiles*
> *As in a looking-glass; and then to sigh, as 'twere*
> *The mort o' th' deer . . .*

Can thy dam?—may't be?—
Affection! thy intention stabs the centre:
Thou dost make possible things not so held,
Communicat'st with dreams;—how can this be?—
With what's unreal thou coactive art,
And fellow'st nothing: then 'tis very credent
Thou may'st co-join with something; and thou dost,
(And that beyond commission) and I find it,
(And that to the infection of my brains
And hard'ning of my brows).

Leontes' speech to Mamillius, mixing what the boy will understand ('Thou want'st a rough pash') with what he won't ('and the shoots that I have To be full like me') is very natural, in its horrible way. So is the talk which ensues, with Polixenes, about their two young princes:

Looking on the lines
Of my boy's face, methoughts I did recoil
Twenty-three years . . .

Leontes is here taking refuge—but also flagellating himself in the process—in the sentimental view of the past, of childhood, which Polixenes invoked earlier in his rather queer address to Hermione on the subject of twinned lambs frisking in the sun, innocent and ignorant of the doctrine of ill-doing. (An address, incidentally, to which Hermione made what seems simultaneously the only possible answer and specifically the answer which Hermione, being what she is, would make.)

The frequent references to childhood, to children, and especially to these particular children, the younger generation, have been noted by most commentators. I would like at this point simply to assert my own view, that, even so, the children are there for the sake of the parents rather than the other way about. No doubt, if winter comes, spring cannot be far behind; but this, I believe, is far more a winter's tale than a tale of spring. The play's special distinction—it is by far, I think, the most powerfully engag-

164

ing of the so-called tragi-comedies—is that it approaches
as near to tragedy as is possible without becoming irrecoverably tragic. There is even a doubt in my mind as to
whether it doesn't at some point cross that mysterious
frontier. At the same time, however, one does not doubt
that the 'avoidance' of the tragic conclusion is legitimately
achieved by the author and is no mere piece of chicanery on
his part or instance of taking the will for the deed on ours.

Hermione has asked her husband, 'Are you mov'd, my
lord?' He replies, with an effect of quickness,

> *No, in good earnest.*
> *How sometimes nature will betray its folly,*
> *Its tenderness, and make itself a pastime*
> *To harder bosoms! Looking on the lines . . .*

This, if I understand it aright, is a rather strange thing to
say in this overtly soft-bosomed company; though of
course it is by no means a strange thing for Leontes to say
to himself, in the company of his new suspicions. He
appears to be urging himself not to display any 'natural'
tenderness, equating tenderness with folly because it makes
one look an awful fool when one's supposed friends turn
out to be enemies, and perhaps warning himself that he
may have to take very untender though sensible steps
against his old friend and his beloved wife. The relapse
into memories of childhood innocence or ignorance, when
even his dagger was muzzled lest it should bite its master,
is altogether natural after this, in addition to seeming quite
natural and reassuring to his mildly worried interrogators
—simply the thoughts of a father out strolling with his
young son.

Leontes' instructions to Hermione on the subject of
Polixenes' entertainment are bound to sound ominous to us,
though (again) they will sound natural to those on the stage:

> *How thou lov'st us, show in our brother's welcome;*
> *Let what is dear in Sicily be cheap . . .*

As he says, he is angling now, 'though you perceive me not how I give line'. This is the cunning of the suspicious man, the self-congratulatory way in which, with conscious shrewdness, he sets about confirming his suspicions. Since others have made a fool of him by hiding something from him, he will now make greater fools of them by finding them out. In the feverishness which is part of his condition—since your enemies had the start of you in committing the act of betrayal, you must travel very fast to overtake them: every minute lost now has the force of an extra adultery—he is naturally quick to reach confirmation:

> *Gone already!*
> *Inch-thick, knee-deep; o'er head and ears a fork'd one.*
> *Go, play, boy, play: thy mother plays, and I*
> *Play too; but so disgrac'd a part, whose issue*
> *Will hiss me to my grave . . .*
>   *There have been,*
> *(Or I am much deceiv'd) cuckolds ere now,*
> *And many a man there is (even at this present,*
> *Now, while I speak this) holds his wife by th' arm,*
> *That little thinks she has been sluic'd in's absence*
> *And his pond fish'd by his next neighbour, by*
> *Sir Smile, his neighbour: nay, there's comfort in't,*
> *Whiles other men have gates, and those gates open'd,*
> *As mine, against their will. Should all despair*
> *That have revolted wives, the tenth of mankind*
> *Would hang themselves. Physic for't there's none . . .*
> *No barricado for a belly. Know't,*
> *It will let in and out the enemy,*
> *With bag and baggage: many thousand on's*
> *Have the disease, and feel't not.*

The satisfying play on the word 'play' leads to the thought of his public shame, which is followed by wise reflections on the ubiquity of cuckoldry, whence is derived a foul and feeble sort of comfort. 'Physic for't there's none': no prevention, therefore no fault or defect implied in him. 'No barricado for a belly': the quasi-judicious, quasi-scientific discourse quickly slides into gloating, a contrary process to that of gilding the lily. Further consolation follows: the disease is not fatal, since many thousands have it without knowing, and moreover Leontes is cleverer, because he does know. The corresponding speech of Posthumus in *Cymbeline* ('We are all bastards . . .') is verbose and insipid by comparison.

Camillo's comments on Polixenes' resistance and how it was overcome are unfortunate, and thus register a 'psychological' point in Leontes' favour. As critics have noted, in another context these remarks could have come from Iago. The jealous man doesn't always have to look for proof: sometimes 'proof' is offered him. It is a short step to supposing that Camillo not only noticed that it required Hermione to persuade Polixenes but is also aware of the illicit relationship between them—and a short step therefore to intensified rage and an exacerbated sensitiveness towards trivialities which would normally pass unnoticed. There is so *much* lost ground to make up, too, for Leontes places himself in the stock position of being the last to find out:

> *'tis far gone,*
> *When I shall gust it last.*

At the same time—the mind consumed by jealousy works fast—isn't there a chance that not everybody knows about it, not (for instance) all the servants, because Camillo after all is more than commonly perceptive, so perhaps only he knows about it, or he and a few others, some severals who are quicker to cotton on? Presumably Camillo's reply is comforting in a small way: most people understand that Polixenes is staying longer; the servants would have to be informed of this, but they wouldn't necessarily know *why* he was staying. Why *is* he staying?—

> *To satisfy your highness, and the entreaties*
> *Of our most gracious mistress.*

Camillo cannot understand why his answer should plunge him into obscure disgrace, and so Leontes explains. His analysis of the variety of ways in which Camillo can have failed in his duty—he must be either dishonest, or a coward, or negligent, or a moron—is quite a brilliant operation of the intellect, the activity of a head-piece extraordinary, and Leontes may well congratulate himself on the purity of his logic and the coolness of his mind. No one prizes coolness and logic so much as the man possessed by irrational fury.

Camillo cannot win. His defence of the queen only provokes Leontes into attacking more fiercely, into making declarations which are less and less retractable and advancing as solid evidence suppositions and speculations which are only that moment entering his head. This is unforgettable, Shakespeare performing at the height of his powers:

> *Is whispering nothing?*
> *Is leaning cheek to cheek? is meeting noses?*
> *Kissing with inside lip? stopping the career*
> *Of laughter with a sigh (a note infallible*
> *Of breaking honesty)? horsing foot on foot?*
> *Skulking in corners? wishing clocks more swift?*
> *Hours, minutes? noon, midnight? and all eyes*
> *Blind with the pin and web, but theirs; theirs only.*
> *That would unseen be wicked? is this nothing?*

The 'proof' of Leontes' contention, the clinching argument, lies in a fine example of utterly irrational reasoning, the kind of rhetoric which is difficult to refute when it comes from somebody else, let alone when it comes from oneself:

> *is this nothing?*
> *Why then the world, and all that's in't, is nothing,*
> *The covering sky is nothing, Bohemia nothing,*
> *My wife is nothing, nor nothing have these nothings,*
> *If this be nothing.*

Quod erat demonstrandum. Having confirmed his suspicions and proved his case against the guilty pair, Leontes
now has the right to treat himself to a little self-pity. If
he had any servants about him who cared as much for his
honour as they do for their pay-packets, they would rid
him of this adulterous enemy. And Camillo now—his
cup-bearer—Camillo (who furthermore owes a lot to him)
is the obvious servant to carry out the job, especially as
(more clearly than any other servant) he can see how
acutely his poor master is suffering . . .

Camillo's incredulity draws from Leontes another perfect piece of reasonableness. Does Camillo seriously believe that Leontes has deliberately imagined a state of
affairs of which he is himself the first and chief victim? Is
it likely that he would wantonly foul his own nest? Would
he set out to bring scandal upon the young son he so
loves? Camillo can only answer, 'I must believe you, sir.'
It should be noted that a concession is thereby obtained:
once Polixenes is disposed of, no action shall be taken
against the queen—if Leontes keeps his word.

The rest of this scene is taken up with necessary
business—Camillo acquaints Polixenes with the situation
and they plan their escape—and the business is conducted
efficiently, in a concise style and a very proper manner.
That is all that need be said of it. But what has gone before
exists on an altogether higher level of achievement, remote as could be from a Shakespeare who was 'tired' or
'bored', and even remoter from a Shakespeare who was
mellowly tranquil. We are already asking ourselves, after
such revilement, what forgiveness? After such collapse,
what possibility of reconstruction? The play is already so
much closer to *Othello* than to *Much Ado about Nothing*—
try to think of switching the titles!—or to *Cymbeline*,
where the hectic convolutions of the plot and the continuous need to clarify them leave little room for anything
to be worked out with intensity or in depth. Or, I would

add, to *The Tempest*, a play whose much-admired 'technical perfection' is secured at the cost of inordinate magic in the action and considerable tedium in the audience.

But there is one passage which stands out in the latter part of the scene, spoken by Polixenes:

> *This jealousy*
> *Is for a precious creature: as she's rare,*
> *Must it be great; and, as his person's mighty,*
> *Must it be violent; and as he does conceive*
> *He is dishonour'd by a man which ever*
> *Profess'd to him; why, his revenges must*
> *In that be made more bitter.*

More than anything else said, this goes a long way towards, not 'redeeming' Leontes, but at least to preserving him as a figure who can conceivably redeem himself eventually—as, in other words, a man for whom we are able to feel that measure of sympathy without which this play would indeed be a fairy-tale in the most belittling sense of the term. Without this reminder, it would be possible for us to forget that while the fact that Polixenes is his boyhood friend makes his jealousy seem all the more 'irrational' or improbable, at the same time it makes his ferocity all the more comprehensible. As does of course the reminder that Hermione is 'a precious creature': if Leontes didn't love her enough not to be jealous, at least he loved her too much to be lightly jealous. The phrase seems little to say for her, but that is because she is going to speak for herself before long, directly and cogently.

Indirectly and in a minor way, it also operates in favour of Leontes that Polixenes and Camillo should make their escape so expeditiously, leaving Hermione (though it is difficult to see how their continued presence would help her) to her fate:

> *Fear o'ershades me:*
> *Good expedition be my friend, and comfort*
> *The gracious queen . . .*

Polixenes is in mortal danger in Sicilia, but the theory that his running away may somehow make it easier for the queen to establish her innocence or to live with Leontes' persuasion of her guilt—if that is what the lines mean— does not induce us to admire him.

ACT II SCENE I

Mamillius is almost as trying as Macduff's son (though we take Mr. Pafford's point, that 'the episode is one of happiness': and we can forgive Shakespeare for conferring an unnatural liveliness on boys who are going to die so young), and we sympathise with the First Lady when she reminds Mamillius that he is soon to have a rival for their favours.

It is understandable, as I have remarked, that Leontes should interpret the surreptitious departure of Polixenes and Camillo as confirmation of Hermione's guilt—which hardly needed further confirmation, but one can't have too much of a good thing. He trusted Hermione, he trusted Polixenes, he trusted Camillo—his betrayal is now threefold. There is some satisfaction in finding yourself even more right than you had thought:

> *How blest am I*
> *In my just censure! in my true opinion!*
> *Alack, for lesser knowledge! how accurs'd*
> *In being so blest! There may be in the cup*
> *A spider steep'd, and one may drink, depart,*
> *And yet partake no venom (for his knowledge*
> *Is not infected); but if one present*
> *Th' abhorr'd ingredient to his eye, make known*
> *How he hath drunk, he cracks his gorge, his sides,*
> *With violent hefts. I have drunk, and seen the spider.*

This is another superb example of logic, of a logical con-struction of thought which, though it is founded on a

delusion, could hardly be less 'frantic'. Leontes is blest,
yet he is accurs'd (and, in truth, he is). The spider in your
cup which you don't see doesn't hurt you. He has been
made a fool of, and then he has been made a fool of again
by Polixenes' escape from his vengeance. This is all very
painful—but at the same time little is so gratifying to the
self-deluded as the contemplation of their own expert
ratiocination. Who said that Shakespeare wasn't a
psychologist?

It is now that Hermione first reveals herself unmistakably as what she is:

> *How will this grieve you,*
> *When you shall come to clearer knowledge, that*
> *You thus have publish'd me! Gentle my lord,*
> *You scarce can right me throughly, then, to say*
> *You did mistake.*

She gives Leontes fair and firm warning. But he is quite
incapable of distinguishing between the foundation and
the edifice which he has so scrupulously erected upon it:

> *No: if I mistake*
> *In those foundations which I build upon,*
> *The centre is not big enough to bear*
> *A school-boy's top.*

Hermione is logical and cool, too, and also right:

> *There's some ill planet reigns:*
> *I must be patient till the heavens look*
> *With an aspect more favourable.*

Since Leontes has told the attendant lords what they had
better not say if they want to stay alive, Hermione tells
them what they had better think if they want to be right.
This made clear, and the king being the king, then 'the
king's will be perform'd'. When she says,

> *this action I now go on*
> *Is for my better grace,*

she strikes the tragic note with a sureness and clarity that I cannot find elsewhere in these last plays.

When Antigonus and another Lord seek to defend Hermione—and incidentally perhaps what Antigonus means is that he would rather have gelded himself at the start than father daughters who 'should not produce fair issue'—Leontes abandons his cool logic and simply abuses them: he doesn't need their advice, it is his own affair, and anyway he is king. He recovers himself to some extent when he admits that he hasn't actually witnessed the adultery—though this is not much of an admission since even today, with the advantage of telephotography, etc., so plain a proof is rarely advanced in divorce courts—and informs the company that in a case like this ''twere most piteous to be wild' and therefore, with his customary level-headedness, he has sent to consult that pre-eminently authoritative witness, the Oracle of Apollo, 'whose spiritual counsel had, Shall stop or spur me'. 'Have I done well?' he asks rhetorically. 'Well done, my lord,' replies a lord.

SCENE II

Paulina is formidable, more than a bit of a shrew; but she will need to be all of this:

> These dangerous, unsafe lunes i' th' king, beshrew
>   them!
> He must be told on't, and he shall: the office
> Becomes a woman best. I'll take 't upon me:
> If I prove honey-mouth'd, let my tongue blister,
> And never to my red-look'd anger be
> The trumpet any more.

She is right: it would be difficult to imagine anyone but a woman, and a woman like Paulina, carrying out the 'office' in the form that it is to take. Just as Emilia has well and succinctly described Hermione in her present state, 'one so great and so forlorn', so she describes Paulina for us: 'Your honour and your goodness is so evident . . .' And what she here leaves unmentioned, Paulina herself advises us of: 'I'll use that tongue I have.' Her powers of persuasion succeed with the Gaoler.

SCENE III

Nor night, nor day, no rest: it is but weakness
To bear the matter thus: mere weakness . . .

The equivocal pleasures of the hunt for 'certainty' are over, and now Leontes must do something to implement his certainty of Hermione's guilt. Traces of the logical process persist in his thinking, mean though it is. He cannot sleep, he is unable to punish Polixenes and Camillo who 'make their pastime at my sorrow', but Hermione is within his power, and her death should therefore restore half his normal sleep to him. Mr. Traversi has a good passage on the exacerbating impotence of Leontes, which he compares with Lear's 'I will do such things . . .', and, as regards the idea that action against Hermione will bring repose, with 'the fallacious search for peace undertaken by Macbeth'.

Ingenuity is to be guarded against, since the concentration of the attention on minor points and small significances can have the effect of blinding the reader to larger matters and arresting the general flow of meaning in his mind. I think Professor Wilson Knight's proposition that in the play's opening scene 'the simplicities of Bohemia are contrasted with the luxuries of Sicilia' is a case in point. Two courtiers are being courtly, and that is all, I would say. For nowhere is there any suggestion that

Hermione or Paulina has been spoilt in the slightest
degree by high living, or that luxury is a pre-requisite to
fits of jealous fury. But what is unfortunate about the proposition is that it is really a piece of hindsight wisdom
deriving from and then read back as confirming the neatly
packaged conception of the play which confronts the 'bad'
court scenes with the 'good' country scenes, the corrupt
or defeated old people with the healthy and triumphant
young ones.

Even so, I venture to point to several possible small
significances which seem to me to contribute to the general
impression I have that the play is a good deal less loosely
constructed than some of its commentators, including
admirers, have made out.

'The harlot king', says Leontes,

> *Is quite beyond mine arm, out of the blank*
> *And level of my brain: plot-proof: but she*
> *I can hook to me.*

In her fine lines in Act III Scene ii, Hermione is to point
out that it is not the level of his brain that her life stands
in, but the level of his dreams. Leontes goes on to say, of
Polixenes,

> *let him be*
> *Until a time may serve.*

It will be a long time indeed, but it will serve: Leontes is
to espouse the cause of the runaway Florizel against his
father. Paulina too has some remarks which I think a
more legitimate hindsight wisdom can find pertinently
resonant. When Antigonus and the others try to prevent
her entering with the baby by telling her that Leontes
has not slept, she says, 'I come to bring him sleep.' She is
to be instrumental in bringing him to the service of repentance, which is not sleep, yet in a sense can be thought of as
sixteen years of a sort of sleep, of life which is not living.

Similarly, Leontes speaks better than he knows when he cries out petulantly,

> *Away with that audacious lady! Antigonus,*
> *I charg'd thee that she should not come about me.*
> *I knew she would.*

He is to have her about him for sixteen years: perhaps he is less unlike Macbeth than one had thought and, even in the mid-stream of error, he has some conception of what the fruits of his error are to be. Paulina describes her future function when she seeks to persuade Leontes of her present purpose:

> *I beseech you hear me, who professes*
> *Myself your loyal servant, your physician,*
> *Your most obedient counsellor, yet that dares*
> *Less appear so, in comforting your evils,*
> *Than such as most seem yours . . .*

She threatens to scratch out the eyes of anyone who touches her: her poor husband (who is clearly warned by her—

> *For ever*
> *Unvenerable be thy hands, if thou*
> *Tak'st up the princess, by that forced baseness*
> *Which he has put upon 't!*)

is to suffer not at her nails, though, but at those of a bear. Lest we should conceive of her as a termagant wholly and solely, Paulina is given, among her plain speaking, a faint touch of that gentleness and temperate tone which she preserves throughout:

> *I'll not call you tyrant;*
> *But this most cruel usage of your queen—*
> *Not able to produce more accusation*
> *Than your own weak-hing'd fancy—something savours*
> *Of tyranny . . .*

If we see her as a termagant, then we might tend to blame her in part for Leontes' intransigence and what it leads to;

though of course there are other reasons why we must see her, in the future, as something much more exalted than an honest, good-hearted and well-meaning shrew.

There is something grimly contemporary about Leontes' words at the close of the scene:

> *Summon a session, that we may arraign*
> *Our most disloyal lady; for, as she hath*
> *Been publicly accus'd, so shall she have*
> *A just and open trial. While she lives*
> *My heart will be a burden to me.*

ACT III SCENE I

Obviously the island of Delphos is a better place to be in at the moment than the court of Sicilia; and 'the ear-deaf'ning voice o' th' Oracle', however startling, is preferable to the dire and tortuous utterances of Leontes. Standing in for a normal though all-too-late recognition by Leontes of his wife's innocence, the Oracle strikes me as more acceptable than Prospero's magic and his helper, Ariel, who appears to have strayed into the play from *A Midsummer Night's Dream*.

SCENE II

Hermione is a Cordelia who considers it her duty *not* to remain silent even while she recognises the uselessness of speaking—and the ridiculousness and humiliation of it:

> *here standing*
> *To prate and talk for life and honour 'fore*
> *Who please to come and hear.*

All the same, she makes a splendid defence counsel,

though she knows that the prosecution cannot but win the case:

> *Sir,*
> *You speak a language that I understand not:*
> *My life stands in the level of your dreams,*
> *Which I'll lay down.*

Again we hear, unmistakably, the note of pure tragedy, as it sounds nowhere else in the last plays. It must be said for Leontes that his answer—'Your actions are my dreams'—is as worthy of her declaration as any repudiation possibly could be. He is not the nasty little horror that some critics have held him to be; however wrongly he suffers, however much suffering he brings upon others, he does suffer. There is no chance that we shall weep over him, but these words alone ought to make the critics pause before they commence their apotheosis of the noble young adolescent Florizel, untouched by guilt, but hardly as yet touched by life. The mere idea of Hermione ever being reunited to the Leontes of some interpretations —bitter, foul-minded, impotent, senilely rotten—is utterly repellent, fit only for the middle stretches of a more than usually disgusting 'tragedy of blood'. It is true though, and plain enough, that Leontes will have to pay a very high price to regain the Hermione we see in this scene:

> *To me can life be no commodity;*
> *The crown and comfort of my life, your favour,*
> *I do give lost, for I do feel it gone,*
> *But know not how it went. My second joy,*
> *And first-fruits of my body, from his presence*
> *I am barr'd, like one infectious. My third comfort*
> *(Starr'd most unluckily) is from my breast*
> *(The innocent milk in it most innocent mouth)*
> *Hal'd out to murder; myself on every post*
> *Proclaim'd a strumpet, with immodest hatred*

The child-bed privilege denied, which 'longs
To women of all fashion; lastly, hurried
Here, to this place, i' th' open air, before
I have got strength of limit. Now, my liege,
Tell me what blessings I have here alive,
That I should fear to die? Therefore proceed.
But yet hear this: mistake me not: no life,
I prize it not a straw, but for mine honour,
Which I would free . . .

There is no need for the few extra words proposed by
Coleridge to make the terms of the Oracle more telling.
They already tell enough. 'The king shall live without an
heir, if that which is lost be not found': Paulina's instructions are quite clear, the king must not 'remarry' (that is,
must not resume his marriage) until and unless the lost
babe is recovered. The persuasive quality of the Oracle in
fact lies in its firmness and brevity: it is less than half as
long as the indictment of Hermione was, and (unlike those
of the indictment) its words are short and simple and
direct. Like Hermione, like Paulina, perhaps the Oracle
is a little on the tactless side!

Leontes rejects it as 'mere falsehood'. Mamillius dies.
Leontes sees the light—

> *Apollo's angry, and the heavens themselves*
> *Do strike at my injustice.*

Johnson, it is worth noting, had this to say: 'This
vehement retractation of Leontes, accompanied with the
confession of more crimes than he was suspected of, is
agreeable to our daily experience of the vicissitudes of
violent tempers, and the eruptions of minds oppressed
with guilt.' Though he appears to have considered that
the play had its absurdities, this obviously was not one of
them.

Leontes' recantation is complete—he still displays

something of that logical or catalogical habit of mind—
but of course it is nowhere near enough:

> *Apollo, pardon*
> *My great profaneness 'gainst thine Oracle!*
> *I'll reconcile me to Polixenes,*
> *New woo my queen, recall the good Camillo,*
> *Whom I proclaim a man of truth, of mercy . . .*

His catalogue of his crimes and future reparations, inter-
larded with praise for Polixenes ('my friend', 'my kingly
guest') and enclosing a seemingly rather excessive en-
comium of Camillo ('good', 'a man of truth, of mercy',
'the good mind', 'most humane and fill'd with honour',
'his piety'), makes but the most passing reference to
Hermione, granting her not even a single adjective. She,
he seems to think, is one of the family, and can be expected to take all this unpleasantness in her stride as
simply an accident of domestic life. Perhaps his casual
silence on this point accounts for Paulina's speech (though
she was absent during his pronouncements) which more
than remedies the deficiency:

> *That thou betray'dst Polixenes, 'twas nothing;*
> *That did but show thee, of a fool, inconstant*
> *And damnable ingrateful; nor was't much,*
> *Thou would'st have poison'd good Camillo's honour,*
> *To have him kill a king; poor trespasses,*
> *More monstrous standing by: whereof I reckon*
> *The casting forth to crows thy baby daughter,*
> *To be or none or little; though a devil*
> *Would have shed water out of fire, ere done 't:*
> *Nor is't directly laid to thee the death*
> *Of the young prince, whose honourable thoughts*
> *(Thoughts high for one so tender) cleft the heart*
> *That could conceive a gross and foolish sire*
> *Blemish'd his gracious dam: this is not, no,*
> *Laid to thy answer: but the last—O lords,*

When I have said, cry 'woe!'—the queen, the queen,
The sweet'st, dear'st creature's dead . . .

Her speech, that is to say, is not merely an undertaking in grim irony. It not only reminds Leontes of what he seems to have taken little care of, but it points to what is the worst thing he has done—the true centre of the play. What she says is *literally* true, it has nothing to do with 'symbolism': Mamillius's death matters of course, but it is not crucial; the loss (and eventually the finding) of the baby daughter is not in itself so important; the queen *is* 'the sweet'st, dear'st creature', and Perdita will never oust her from that position. This is not merely the devoted and doting Paulina speaking: it is what Shakespeare, what the whole play, will tell us, I believe.

Critics have commonly run riot in their dealings with the pastoral scenes, finding their central significances there, perhaps because of some private yearning for lost innocence and youth, possibly because of some unconscious urge to make amends for the suffering they have inflicted on the young whom they teach. If they looked at the *poetry* of the play, they might suspect that, even so, despite the rather antiquarian charm of the English countryside, despite the more real charm of Perdita, the force of the play is exerted in different quarters, that the tragic note sounds so much more piercingly than the piping idyllic—and that, to put it coarsely, the older generation carry the day and the tale. Look at Paulina:

Do not repent these things, for they are heavier
Than all thy woes can stir: therefore betake thee
To nothing but despair. A thousand knees
Ten thousand years together, naked, fasting,
Upon a barren mountain, and still winter
In storm perpetual, could not move the gods
To look that way thou wert.

Are we, for the greater glory of some youth-versus-age

formula, or some season-myth, to tell ourselves that the
poetry is 'only poetry'?

In her next speech Paulina seemingly changes her tune:

> *Alas! I have show'd too much*
> *The rashness of a woman: he is touch'd*
> *To th' noble heart. What's gone and what's past help*
> *Should be past grief . . .*

But of course she doesn't believe that what's gone and
what's past help is truly past grief, either as a general principle (I would think) or in its particular application to this
case, where in truth the queen is not gone. So she continues,

> *The love I bore your queen—lo, fool again!*
> *I'll speak of her no more, nor of your children:*
> *I'll not remember you of my own lord*
> *(Who is lost too) . . .*

This is an instance of what Mr. Pafford calls 'the cal-
culating tactlessness which is her favourite weapon'. But
there is another calculation going on in her mind. One of
the lords has already complained of the boldness of her
speech, and she is now seeking Leontes' unambiguous
permission to tell him the truth about his behaviour and
its results—as it were, to obtain his signature on the
licence which will make her his 'gaoler', his *memento mori*,
his spiritual adviser for the future. It is necessary that he
shall invite her of his own free will, and this he does when
he replies,

> *Thou didst speak but well*
> *When most the truth: which I receive much better*
> *Than to be pitied of thee.*

He then concludes,

> *Once a day I'll visit*
> *The chapel where they lie, and tears shed there*
> *Shall be my recreation. So long as nature*
> *Will bear up with this exercise, so long*
> *I daily vow to use it.*

The sad tale has been resumed, which Mamillius had begun to tell:

> *There was a man . . .*
> *Dwelt by a churchyard . . .*

SCENE III

> *. . . the skies look grimly,*
> *And threaten present blusters. In my conscience,*
> *The heavens with that we have in hand are angry,*
> *And frown upon 's.*

There is no need for criticism to tell us that the tempest itself 'carries on, symbolically speaking, the idea of the divine displeasure' when the Mariner has made the point so clearly. The consonance of weather with human behaviour or more commonly misbehaviour is old folk poetry: 'so fair and foul a day . . .'; the British talk about the weather a lot. Evidently the storm has a quite unsymbolical function, in which it is aided by the quite unsymbolical bear.

'Exit, pursued by a bear.' Of course Antigonus could be struck dead by lightning, he could rejoin the ship after depositing the baby and then drown with the rest of them. He could succumb to a heart attack. An eagle could drop a tortoise on his bald head. Or, equally well, he could be pursued and eaten by a bear—indeed, more aptly, it being one of those animals he mentioned earlier as celebrated for their 'offices of pity' to abandoned infants. If any further defence of the bear is required—though there will be no satisfying the student who finds such an exit 'slightly jarring in the case of this good man'—we can call upon Nevill Coghill and his remarks on the mixture of the

183

terrible and (Antigonus being rather tedious) the grotes-
quely comic in the spectacle of a bear carrying off an
elderly gentleman.*

Mr. Traversi maintains that this scene is 'the turning
point of the whole play', 'the point of balance upon which
the whole action turns', and I suppose we can agree with
him if we are simply thinking of the story-line. Otherwise
there seem to me to be far more powerful scenes in the
play and several other (and more momentous) turning
points and points of balance. As one of the latter I would
choose that speech of Paulina's recently quoted:

> *A thousand knees*
> *Ten thousand years together . . .*

But when Mr. Traversi subdivides and tells us that 'the
central remark of the whole scene' is the (admittedly
resonant) remark of the Shepherd, 'thou met'st with
things dying, I with things new-born', we can deduce the
nature of the pattern which he and some other critics have
discovered in the play—discovered in or perhaps imposed
upon, for in my own experience the tendency and growth
of the play lies in another direction altogether. Leontes,
Hermione and Paulina withdraw from the stage but they
do not recede from our memory.

Mr. Traversi opposes what he calls 'the warm, living
"blood" of youth' or 'the summer of youth' to 'the
jealousy and care-laden envy of age' or 'jealous, impotent
age'. Professor Wilson Knight does much the same thing:
'evil passions, storm, and shipwreck are contrasted with
young love and humour . . . Maturity and death are set
against birth and resurrection,' and the play presents 'a
contrast of sinful maturity and nature-guarded youth' and,
more obscurely, 'the "eternal" consciousness of childhood
is distinguished from the sin-born time-consciousness of

* 'Six Points of Stage-Craft in *The Winter's Tale*', *Shakespeare Survey*,
11, 1958.

man'. Quiller-Couch considers that the play 'never fits into our mind as a whole' and 'we think of it in parts': but never mind, there is one good part—Shakespeare 'has so managed it, anyhow, that Florizel and Perdita, no active persons in the drama . . . find themselves the centre of it, being young and natural and therefore in love'. More bleakly, E. M. W. Tillyard allows Leontes and Hermione to live on 'to give continuity to the play', but is quite confident that their 'continued existence is a matter of subordinate expediency; and it is Florizel and Perdita and the countryside where they meet which make the new life'.*

This popular interpretation of the play as a confrontation of old baddies and young goodies, with the former yielding to the latter easily and to their own advantage, ought to be found highly gratifying by modern youth; and most especially, I would think, when couched in the proleptically hippy terminology used by Professor Wilson Knight. 'A contrast of sinful maturity and nature-guarded youth . . .' Trust nobody over—well, to adopt the Shepherd's figure, three-and-twenty. Evidently if one were offered a choice between 'the jealousy and care-laden envy of age' on the one hand and 'the warm, living "blood" of youth' on the other, one would not hesitate. Evidently if one were offered the choice of either Macbeth or Malcolm as one's ruler, one would know which candidate to vote for. But in the plays as we have them, we are infinitely more interested in Macbeth than in Malcolm, and (I contend) far more involved with Leontes and Hermione than with Perdita and Florizel. 'The summer of youth . . . jealous, impotent age': these tendentious expressions are programme notes to some other play than *The Winter's Tale*, for in this play there is nothing so neat as a simple affirmation of the nicer state of affairs against the nastier, and we must follow the poetry, and not some

* *Shakespeare's Last Plays*, 1938.

critic's natural preference for sweetness and light over bitterness and dark.

Since he had decided that somehow or other Florizel and Perdita found themselves the centre of the play, it was inevitable that Quiller-Couch should have regarded the mere reporting of the recognition of Perdita as 'the greatest fault of all'. This is twisting the evidence to fit one's theory, and we should rather understand Shakespeare's choosing to relegate the recognition of Perdita to a reported description, then to interpose a short passage of comedy, and then follow with the great scene of Hermione's discovery, as a plain indication of where he would have the play's heart and centre to be.

Lest my view of the play be ascribed to the evil passions of old age, to jealousy and impotence, I should remark that when I studied *The Winter's Tale* in the sixth form, it was the jealous nausea of Leontes, the nobility and dignified suffering of Hermione and, some way behind, the high moral nursemaiding of Paulina, which held my imagination, whereas I found the pastoral fourth act slow and tedious and mawkish—considerably more so than I do now.

ACT IV SCENE I

Time, the Chorus, puns excessively on his own name, but makes no reference to Professor Wilson Knight's ' "eternal" consciousness', nor does he point to any moral superiority in the younger generation (indeed, he has not tried them yet) or any notable 'regeneration' which they are to bring about. Time is neutral, he both 'makes and unfolds error':

> *let Time's news*
> *Be known when 'tis brought forth.*

My traffic is sheets; when the kite builds, look to lesser linen.
My father named me Autolycus; who, being as I am, littered
under Mercury, was likewise a snapper-up of unconsidered
trifles. With die and drab I purchased this caparison, and my
revenue is the silly cheat . . . for the life to come, I sleep out the
thought of it.

Et in Arcadia ego. Mr. Traversi confesses that he cannot
symbolicise Autolycus, who remains 'a reminder that the
complexity of life is not readily to be reduced to any
symbolic scheme, however generous and inclusive'. Perhaps after all Mr. Traversi has made a symbol of him!—
but a useful one, for if Autolycus were no more than a
powerful reminder of the kind described, he would have
earned a place in the story. He is also the source of considerable entertainment; though, as Professor Wilson
Knight points out, 'the merry robber-tramp, as he makes
his way, becomes less merry'.

Perdita casts Florizel into the shade; he may be a king's
son, but she is Hermione's daughter. When she indicates
her dislike of dressing up (on her part)—though a little
later she is to disguise herself more thoroughly—and of
dressing down (on his), he retorts with a less than modest
speech about the gods and how, 'humbling their deities to
love', they

> *have taken*
> *The shapes of beasts upon them: Jupiter*
> *Became a bull, and bellow'd; the green Neptune*
> *A ram, and bleated; and the fire-rob'd god,*
> *Golden Apollo, a poor humble swain,*
> *As I seem now.*

187

The rest of this speech, in praise of Perdita, is distinctly more persuasive, though the modern reader may be slightly put off by Florizel's talk about his lusts not burning hotter than his faith. Shakespeare liked to make his good young people quite explicitly good in sexual matters, distinguishing them perhaps from the rut of youthful behaviour as observed at all periosd—and in this present one by the Shepherd.

Perdita is realistic; and realism in women is more proper and more touching than in men, where it tends to look suspiciously like pusillanimity. 'To me the difference forges dread': what if his father should happen to pass that way, just as Florizel happened to? When she says,

> *O, but sir,*
> *Your resolution cannot hold when 'tis*
> *Oppos'd, as it must be, by th' power of the king:*
> *One of these two must be necessities,*
> *Which then will speak, that you must change this*
>   *purpose,*
> *Or I my life,*

we recognise the tone of Hermione's voice, arraigned before the court of Sicilia, and I suspect that a good deal of the admiration we feel for Perdita derives by association of this kind from the admiration we have formed for Hermione; to a certain extent the younger woman is living on unearned income, inherited wealth.

The 'great debate' between Perdita and Polixenes on the subject of hybrids hardly deserves the attention it has received. He is right where she is wrong, and worse, a shade prissy about those poor carnations and gillyvors: 'I'll not put The dibble in earth to set one slip of them', so there! It has often been observed that while Polixenes is philosophically in the right, he changes his views when it comes to putting them into practice: he has no intention of allowing his son to 'make conceive a bark of baser kind' by marrying a shepherdess. (He is also right when he remarks,

> *This is the prettiest low-born lass that ever*
> *Ran on the green-sward: nothing she does or seems*
> *But smacks of something greater than herself,*
> *Too noble for this place*

—an intuition which he is soon to thrust aside.) It is the case, too, that Perdita is prepared to act against her botanical principles by uniting herself with 'a gentler scion'; though she, I suppose, can be forgiven her illogic on the grounds that she is swayed by an unconscious conviction that she is quite as good socially as Florizel. But it is all, I would say, a pleasing conversation piece on country matters between a king in disguise and a princess in disguise, and no doubt the listening rustics were properly impressed.

I could never make out—and cannot quite now—what all the talk of flowers and maidenheads is meant to convey. The daffodils (which alas cannot be found in any corner of a foreign field) may pass muster; the violets are (what they are said to be) 'dim'; but I do not know what to make of the

> *pale primroses,*
> *That die unmarried, ere they can behold*
> *Bright Phoebus in his strength (a malady*
> *Most incident to maids)* . . .

Perhaps it was an early distaste for such manifestations of 'nature' which led to this speech almost spoiling the play for me, while

> *lilies of all kinds,*
> *The flower-de-luce being one*

encouraged me in suspicions of interpolation before I had ever heard of the possibility that other hands than Shakespeare's could have been at work in plays attributed to him.

Tillyard (as one might expect from one who only tolerates the oldsters for the sake of continuity) attributes great significance to the verse of the flower speech, which he finds 'leisurely, full, assured, matured, suggestive of fruition, and acutely contrasted to the tortured, arid, and barren ravings of Leontes, and which reinforces . . . kinship with nature and healthy sensuality'. Again, fruition is nicer than barrenness, healthy sensuality than unhealthy loathings, and Malcolm is a nicer man than Macbeth. Leontes' 'ravings' happen to be in rather good verse—Tillyard himself remarked on their 'hot and twisted language'—and they hit us harder than Perdita's flowers, no matter how readily the latter lend themselves to excogitated significances.* As for maturity, assurance and fruition, I would agree with Philip Edwards when he writes, regarding the 'balanced view of life' which has so bewitched critics of the last plays, that 'it is a disservice to Shakespeare to pretend that one is adding to his profundity by discovering that his plots are symbolic vehicles for ideas and perceptions which are, for the most part, banal, trite and colourless'.†

It will be readily granted that the debile effect of this sentimentalised seed-merchant's catalogue—even Mr. Traversi acknowledges a 'lack of vigour' in the primroses —is sharply modified by Perdita's next pronouncement:

> *like a bank, for love to lie and play on:*
> *Not like a corpse; or if—not to be buried,*
> *But quick, and in mine arms.*

And also by her remark that she feels she has been acting a part, 'as I have seen them do In Whitsun pastorals . . .' Looked at in this way, the scene is rather affecting: a

---

* Tillyard is right, I would say, on the subject of Florizel: 'kept a rather flat character the more to show up Perdita . . . for the play's purposes he is an efficient type of chivalry and generosity'.

† 'Shakespeare's Romances: 1900–1957', *Shakespeare Survey, 11.*

young country girl has been seeking to impress a couple of elderly strangers by offering them the sort of perform-ance she supposes they want to see.

'What you do,' answers Florizel, 'Still betters what is done', and

> *Each your doing,*
> *So singular in each particular,*
> *Crowns what you are doing, in the present deeds,*
> *That all your acts are queens.*

This may remind some of us of a greater and more pathetic queen, Cleopatra. It could be the comparative tepidness of the young in this play which throws the door open to the symbol-hunters: if there were more woman in Perdita, we should have less talk of 'grace', and if there were more blood in Florizel we should hear less about 'blood'. When Mr. Traversi claims that here we have 'a world less limited to the merely personal, more universal and symbolic in its implications' than the world of *Antony and Cleopatra*, he seems to me merely to be bringing his conception of the symbolic into disrepute. If you believe that all young people are the same young people, then certainly any young person will do to symbolise all other young people—and the whole lot of them, young people and symbols alike, very soon become just a bore. It is sheer philistinism to throw out intensely realised char-acters, such as the 'merely personal' Antony and Cleo-patra, in order to make room for 'universal' types.

In his interpretation of the flower scene and its symbol-ism or 'symbolic motives' Mr. Traversi seems to suggest that Perdita knows all that has happened as well as all that is to happen. Granted the action in her of nature, such preternatural knowledge is still incongruous in a princess who has been nurtured as a shepherdess and believes her-self to be one. But it must be said for Mr. Traversi that he pushes on, just as the play does. The section on *The*

Winter's Tale in Middleton Murry's book about Shakespeare is almost entirely devoted to the pastoral scenes and
more particularly the flower passages: Murry finds
Leontes' jealousy 'extravagant' and dismisses Hermione's
appearance in the guise of a statue as 'a theatrical trick'.

Polixenes is bound to be angered by his son's cryptic
(and vain-glorious) reply to the Shepherd's promise to
make his daughter's portion equal to the young man's:

> *O, that must be*
> *I' th' virtue of your daughter: one being dead,*
> *I shall have more than you can dream of yet;*
> *Enough then for your wonder.*

The king's preamble—

> *Methinks a father*
> *Is at the nuptial of his son a guest*
> *That best becomes the table*

—is sober and reasonable, and he offers his son (sincerely
or not) a chance to put things right: 'Let him know 't
. . . Prithee, let him.' It has been suggested that Elizabethan audiences would feel considerable sympathy for
Polixenes, not only because he is an unconsulted father
but because he is a king, and a king's son is a sceptre's
heir and not, on the face of it, to be encouraged to affect
a sheep-hook. But his reaction exceeds the legitimate,
even the kingly, and we can only feel disgust at his proposal (quickly dropped) to hang the Shepherd—who had
agreed with him that the young man's father ought to be
acquainted with the business, adding sagely that 'he shall
not need to grieve At knowing of thy choice'—and his
threat to have Perdita's beauty 'scratch'd with briers'. In
fact all he does is forbid further meetings between the
two, as many an irate parent has done, though in this case
on pain of death to the girl. Our natural egalitarianism

(generally more active in art than in reality) and our dislike of noise tell us what to feel about this—and I dare say
it is not much different from what Elizabethan audiences
felt.

At the same time I cannot agree with Mr. Traversi that
'it is clear that Polixenes has fallen into a course of
passionate error scarcely less disastrous, in its way, than
that which has already destroyed Leontes' peace'. All
error is to be deplored, of course, but some errors are
altogether more disastrous than others: and Polixenes'
error is to prove quite a happy fault. At no point does it
become a very unhappy one in its effects. This spot of
unpleasantness is aptly placed by Autolycus when he
talks of the old man coming in 'with a whoo-bub against
his daughter and the king's son' and spoiling his day's
business. We cannot for a moment imagine anyone saying
anything remotely like this about Leontes' accusation of
Hermione. The author has placed his pointers—but reading too much into Shakespeare generally goes along with
not reading enough of Shakespeare.

We cannot but admire Perdita when she says, after the
king's petulant exit,

> *Even here, undone,*
> *I was not much afeard; for once or twice*
> *I was about to speak, and tell him plainly,*
> *The selfsame sun that shines upon his court*
> *Hides not his visage from our cottage, but*
> *Looks on alike.*

The idea, as the editors have pointed out, is both proverbial (the wisdom, or the consolation, of the lower
orders) and scriptural (equal shares for all of that pie in
the sky). Yet the speech will seem hardly more than pert
if we set it side by side with Hermione's lines, 'My life
stands in the level of your dreams . . .' Perdita was 'about
to speak'; Hermione did speak.

N   193

What follows is admirable, too, and impressively adult:

> *Will't please you, sir, be gone?*
> *I told you what would come of this: beseech you,*
> *Of your own state take care: this dream of mine—*
> *Being now awake, I'll queen it no inch farther,*
> *But milk my ewes, and weep.*

Florizel's rather belated expression of resoluteness of purpose ('what I was, I am . . .') is schoolboyish in comparison. Perdita renounces her dream, she is ready to live without it, to milk her ewes and weep. Hermione was prepared to die because of someone else's dream. Perdita is a healthy girl and, fair enough, she exhibits 'moral integrity', as Mr. Traversi says; but Hermione is a tragic figure.

The Shepherd's words, if one recalls Macbeth's similar declaration, are merely comic, and the more so if we assume that he didn't realise he had been reprieved:

> *If I might die within this hour, I have liv'd*
> *To die when I desire,*

while Florizel's oath,

> *Let nature crush the sides o' th' earth together,*
> *And mar the seeds within!*

sounds like a tired version of something more congruously uttered by Lear or Macbeth: it is a fine thing if Doomsday is to be brought upon us by a frustrated young lover!

Camillo arranges for the two young people to escape to Sicilia. He then proposes to himself to betray them to the king so that Polixenes and he shall chase the runaways and

> *I shall re-view Sicilia, for whose sight*
> *I have a woman's longing.*

194

Very smart! Yet, apropos of Florizel's remark that
what Camillo purposes is 'almost a miracle', Mr. Traversi writes thus: 'the phrase, indicating that there is
about Camillo himself at this stage "something more than
man", suggests the presence of the divine working behind
his project'. Divinity works in a mysterious way, as they
say, and it could be argued that it is working behind
Autolycus too, since the princess's fardel is practically as
important as the princess herself. Mr. Traversi has a long
and rapturous passage about the welcome Camillo en-
visages Florizel receiving from Leontes—

> *Methinks I see*
> *Leontes opening his free arms and weeping*
> *His welcomes forth*

—and all its symbolism. To the cooler judgment, however, it will appear that at the best Camillo is planning to
exploit Leontes' remorse on the subject of Polixenes by
implying an untruth about Florizel's relations with his
father, and at the worst he is simply serving his own turn.

We do not blame Camillo, for we can sympathise with
his wish to go home, but I shouldn't have thought we
would feel inclined to erect him into some godlike figure
or divine front. All that sharp operators symbolise is sharp
operating. 'What a fool Honesty is! and Trust, his
sworn brother, a very simple gentleman!' We feel a
twinge of pity for the young couple, and perhaps a touch
of scorn too when we hear the simple prince addressing
Camillo in Malcolm-like terms as 'the medicine of our
house', even though the description will turn out correct.
But we are content to go along with Camillo, and leave the
morality of the situation unexplored, for the simple and
strong reason that we too (unless we look for flowers all
the way) want to get back to Sicilia. With Shakespeare a
little pastoral customarily goes a long way.

ACT V SCENE I

Sir, you have done enough, and have perform'd
A saint-like sorrow: no fault could you make,
Which you have not redeem'd; indeed, paid down
More penitence than done trespass: at the last,
Do as the heavens have done, forget your evil;
With them, forgive yourself.

I cannot agree with Mr. Pafford in his contention that 'Leontes shows little sign of spiritual or moral growth.' He adds, 'In so far as Shakespeare intends to give him personality Leontes is really a picture of a rather ordinary man all the time and at the end of the play an ageing man, who indeed ought to be even older than his years.' Leontes is not a Lear or a Macbeth, nor was he meant to be: that is plain enough. But neither is he as inconsiderable as the phrase 'a rather ordinary man' would have him be. I get the strong impression in Act v of a man who has suffered and is truly contrite. Understandably Shakespeare does not show him crawling on his belly for half an hour at a stretch. But the 'growth', the difference in spiritual stature from the man we saw in the earlier part of the play, is conveyed clearly and cogently in the tone of voice with which he now speaks. In his answer to Cleomenes, one of those despatched to the Oracle, if we don't see him performing penances we do see him refusing to lay them aside:

Whilst I remember
Her, and her virtues, I cannot forget
My blemishes in them, and so still think of
The wrong I did myself: which was so much,
That heirless it hath made my kingdom, and
Destroy'd the sweet'st companion that e'er man
Bred his hopes out of.

The punishment is a continuing one, that is, it cannot be remitted. And we take note of his quick and still raw response to Paulina's sustained tactlessness:

> *Kill'd!*
> *She I kill'd! I did so: but thou strik'st me*
> *Sorely, to say I did: it is as bitter*
> *Upon thy tongue as in my thought. Now, good now,*
> *Say so but seldom.*

The danger, we might think, is that we shall find a man who has been completely broken by remorse and Paulina. And it is one of Shakespeare's inimitable touches that Leontes should look on Perdita with an eye that (Paulina quickly points out) 'hath too much youth in 't', and so reassure us that the process of regeneration hasn't quite finished him off. There must be something left for Hermione to come back to.

Much more repentance put in Leontes' mouth would merely bore us, or perhaps arouse a suspicion that the gentleman protests too much; signs of 'spiritual or moral growth' must be kept discreet and indirect if they are not to defeat their purpose and repel the spectator. And in any case, if anyone is to be allowed to be a saint, it must be Hermione, not Leontes. But he is given sufficient to say: 'No more such wives; therefore, no wife' are not exactly words we would expect to hear from a rather ordinary man, and nor are

> *Stars, stars,*
> *And all eyes else, dead coals!*

Formidable as we guess—indeed, as we see—her to be, Paulina is still endearing. Not only is she the keeper of the king's conscience, she is the public custodian of the memory of Hermione's beauty. She loves Hermione above and beyond any call of duty to the Oracle or the demands of any ethical system, as is amusingly brought out when she turns upon the Servant, a verse-scribbling gentleman who forgets himself sufficiently to praise a parvenue princess in her presence. Failing to put down the Servant at all firmly, she turns on Leontes and reminds him of Mamillius, who would have paired well with this newly arrived prince.

Now, inevitably, there will be much talk, happy and sad, about the younger generation, and I don't think we really need to debate the question of whether they are gathered here for their own sakes or for the sake of fulfilling the Oracle and releasing the sleeping queen. Finally there is no real division between young and old, certainly no competition between them for symbolic supremacy. If I have here taken the side of 'the old people', it was in order to rectify the perverse imbalance of so much recent criticism; it was not to sweep the young off the stage, but to affirm my conviction that, whoever else may join them there, Hermione and Leontes (and I would add Paulina) stand in the centre of the stage, at the heart of our involvement, and are kept there by the tensions of the play's most urgent and most delicate poetry.

SCENE II

I have given the reason, as I see it, why the recognition of Perdita is reported to the audience instead of acted before it. One climax on stage would detract from the other: and the discovery of Hermione is the climax of Shakespeare's play. Nevertheless, the reporting is done very well: everything in need of explanation is explained clearly and quite briskly, despite the somewhat ornate delivery, and everybody (including the shade of Hermione) is introduced into the account. Paulina, in fact, is quite dramatically present to us in the Third Gentleman's prose:

> She had one eye declined for the loss of her husband, another elevated that the Oracle was fulfilled: she lifted the princess from the earth, and so locks her in embracing as if she would pin her to her heart, that she might no more be in danger of losing.

If this procedure is a second-best, it is still remarkably good, and it ranks high among recognition scenes in literature of any genre.

The unveiling of the work of the rare Italian master is prepared for; and, for there is first to be a passage of comic relief and dramatic delay in the company of Autolycus, the Shepherd and the Clown, our excitement is sustained in adroit fashion by the First Gentleman's hint:

> Every wink of an eye, some new grace will be born: our absence makes us unthrifty to our knowledge. Let's along.

SCENE III

At one extreme (Middleton Murry), the statue scene is 'a theatrical trick'; at the other (Mr. Traversi), 'it is not an accident that Hermione's slow re-awakening . . . is from now on surrounded by symbols explicitly religious'. More congenial than either, I find, is the cooler attitude indicated in Mr. Pafford's remark that 'the scene is primarily a straight-forward elucidation of the mystery'. Rather than esoteric or mysterious, the scene is brightly lucid, chaste in its simplicity, classically sculptural throughout—but far from naive. It communicates and reveals through movements, stillnesses, words and silences; and, far from being symbolic and standing for something else, it stands for itself, it appears to be the thing itself, which a lesser author would have gone to considerable pains to symbolise simply because he was incapable of this fine immediacy.

At once Leontes perceives a difference between the statue and Hermione, or Hermione as he remembers her:

> *But yet, Paulina,*
> *Hermione was not so much wrinkled, nothing*
> *So aged as this seems.*

Here is realism again. The wrinkles are to remind us, as well as Leontes, that sixteen real years have passed, that this is to be no resuscitation of a supposedly dead Juliet before a live Romeo, that Hermione is not the Sleeping Beauty and *The Winter's Tale* is no fairy story.

There is even a touch of the humorous in Paulina's stage-managing—this is her great day—and especially in her discouraging of both Leontes' and Perdita's impulse to kiss the statue:

> *O patience!*
> *The statue is but newly fix'd, the colour's*
> *Not dry*

—a little more patience is asked for, after sixteen years of patience. We see how fitting it is that Perdita's reaction to the statue should be so simple, in contrast to the complexity of Leontes' state of mind. And we note how proprietary Paulina's attitude towards Hermione still is: 'the stone is mine'; and also how Leontes' gratitude to her for this sight of his wife is mixed with cajolery: 'O sweet Paulina . . .'

Professor Wilson Knight has mentioned the resemblance between Leontes' speech,

> *Still methinks*
> *There is an air comes from her. What fine chisel*
> *Could ever yet cut breath? Let no man mock me,*
> *For I will kiss her,*

and Lear's words, when his daughter is restored to him:

> *Do not laugh at me;*
> *For, as I am a man, I think this lady*
> *To be my child Cordelia.*

There is also a resemblance with Lear's later words,

> *This feather stirs; she lives! if it be so,*
> *It is a chance which does redeem all sorrows*
> *That ever I have felt,*

and with his last words,

> *Do you see this? Look on her, look, her lips,*
> *Look there, look there!*

The statue comes alive: this is the death of Cordelia in reverse. One is conscious of course of all the huge differences, but I think it is true (and if so, it is very remarkable) that here, at the close of what is *not* a tragedy, in fact at the very moment of reconciliation, there are distinct intimations of tragedy, the tragic vein still runs visibly through something which is so much lighter.

Perhaps what Mr. Traversi sees as explicitly religious references surrounding the return of Hermione are chiefly Paulina's references to magic, her simulated fear that she might be thought to be 'assisted By wicked powers', and her insistence on the whiteness of her art, the lawfulness of her 'spell'. Rather than the imparting to the scene of a religious dimension of some sort (and what sort, one wonders: Christ coming down from the Cross, the raising of Lazarus?), this is Paulina's pertinent emphasis on the legitimacy of what she is doing (that is, restoring Hermione to her husband at the earliest—or not much later than the earliest—lawful moment), a repudiation of the black-magical acts we encounter elsewhere in the theatre (for example, the calling up of Helen's shade to satisfy Faustus's lust), and also a simple device for maintaining and enhancing the suspense. Mr. Traversi talks of 'the

essentially religious nature of the action we are witnessing': essentially the action is human in nature, I believe,
the 'religious symbols' (if such there be) bear a human
meaning. Leontes—and this is an excellent touch—
doesn't care in the least what colour Paulina's art is!

Altogether secular and realistic is the way Hermione
doesn't speak to Leontes and yet there is 'speech in their
dumbness'. They embrace, and otherwise they com-
municate through Paulina or their daughter. Then the
play ends with a brisk speech from Leontes, a tying up of
loose ends. Paulina, her occupation gone, starts to mourn
for her lost mate and for herself, but she is quickly
silenced by Leontes, who has taken the reins of govern-
ment back into his own hands:

> *O, peace, Paulina!*
> *Thou shouldst a husband take by my consent,*
> *As I by thine a wife: this is a match,*
> *And made between 's by vows . . .*
> > *Come, Camillo,*
> *And take her by the hand . . .*

'Camillo has acquired a wife beyond price', says Mr.
Pafford. And perhaps, we suspect, beyond his means.
But not for a moment would we want her really to wing
herself to some wither'd bough, and we guess that she
doesn't really want to, either. Her place is at court, and
she will always find occupation there.

*   *   *

We experience relief, pleasure and deep satisfaction
that something which it seemed could only come to a
melancholy conclusion is ending, certainly not in an orgy
of rejoicing, but in a quietly happy reunion. That we
should feel this way is not due to any innate and over-
whelming preference on our part for happy endings: how

should we react if Cordelia did open her eyes and rise to her feet? That the 'happy ending' of *The Winter's Tale* is right is the result of the other parts of the play being what, in conjunction, they are. The artistic logic which brings us lawfully to this ending is too delicate, too complex, for analysis: in a case of this nature it is not so much that we murder to dissect as that we look very silly doing it. That we are assured of the logic or the legitimacy of the conclusion at the conclusion, may well depend upon our not being intellectually conscious of the logical steps the play makes *en route*. For so, the play's close is both magical and lawful, unexpected at the time and inevitable a moment later.

INDEX